Collins
English for Exams

Get Ready for IELTS
READING

Els Van Geyte

Collins

HarperCollins Publishers
The News Building
1 London Bridge Street
London
SE1 9GF

First edition 2012

© HarperCollins Publishers 2012

ISBN 978–0–00–746064–9

Collins® is a registered trademark of HarperCollins Publishers Limited

www.collinselt.com

A catalogue record for this book is available from the British Library

Typeset in India by Aptara

Printed in China by RR Donnelley APS.

Photo credits

All photos from Shutterstock

cover: **Andresr**; p8: **Mira Bavutti Deganello**; p8: **Zurijeta**; p14: **sjgh**; p14: **Miro Kovacevic**; p14: **Sean Gladwell**; p14: **ollyy**; p20: **valeriya_sh**; p20: **Lorraine Swanson**; p27: **pjcross**; p27: **nakamasa**; p27: **Iakov Kalinin**; p28: **photo25th**; p28: **Aleksandr Bryliaev**; p28: **Khomulo Anna**; p28: **Ivica Drusany**; p31: **DeSerg**; p32: **Everyday smiles**; p32: **Ruth Black**; p34: **PHB.cz (Richard Semik)**; p34: **Peter Wey**; p34: **Pete Saloutos**; p34: **mirrormere**; p38: **wonderisland**; p40: **RetroClipArt**; p40: **Johan Knelsen**; p40: **Johan Knelsen**; p47: **psamtik**; p47: **Borzee**; p48: **brinkstock**; p48: **Ryan R Fox**; p52: **Arcady**; p60: **daseaford**; p60: **mangostock**; p60: **Ken Schulze**; p67: **Roxana Gonzalez**; p67: **ra2studio**; p67: **Monkey Business Images**; p67: **daseaford**; p68: **David Burrows**; p68: **Renata Sedmakova**; p68: **BasPhoto**; p74: **Ruslan Kuzmenkov**; p74: **Szasz-Fabian Ilka Erika**; p80: **Tamara Kulikova**; p80: **Jeff Dalton**; p80: **Efired**; p80: **Stephen Finn**; p80: **Svinkin**

About the author

Els Van Geyte has been working at the English for International Students Unit at the University of Birmingham (UK) for over 10 years, teaching IELTS exam strategies and the academic language skills her students need for their chosen courses. She is also the author of *Reading for IELTS* (Collins, 2011).

Contents

Introduction

Who is this book for?

Get Ready for IELTS Reading has been written for learners with a band score of 3 or 4 who want to achieve a higher score. Using this book will help you improve your pre-intermediate reading skills for the IELTS Academic Reading test.

You can use *Get Ready for IELTS Reading*:

- as a self-study course. We recommend that you work systematically through the 12 units in order to benefit from its progressive structure.
- as a supplementary reading skills course for IELTS preparation classes. The book provides enough material for approximately 50 hours of classroom activity.

Get Ready for IELTS Reading

- This book consists of **12 units**. Each unit focuses on a different topic and these topics are ones that often appear in the IELTS exam.
- After every three units, there is a **Review unit** which helps you to revise the language and skills covered in the previous units.
- At the end of the book the **Practice test** gives you the opportunity to take an IELTS-style test under test conditions.
- There is also a full **Answer key** at the back of the book so you can check your answers. Here you will find suggested answers for more open-ended questions and model answers for the exam practice questions in Part 3 of the unit.
- The **Glossary** at the back of the book lists the useful words from each unit with their Cobuild dictionary definitions.

Unit structure

Each unit starts with the **Aims** of the unit. They outline the key language and skills covered.

Part 1: Language development provides exercises on vocabulary related to the topic as well as any relevant grammar points related to the IELTS Task covered in the unit. Clear structures are provided.

Part 2: Skills development provides information and practice on the task types you will come across in the IELTS Reading test. An explanation of each task type is followed by exercises of increasing difficulty. These exercises give you the opportunity to practise the skills that are needed to complete the task, and they help you to develop strategies for completing these tasks in the test.

Part 3: Exam practice provides realistic exam practice questions for the tasks you have been practising, in a format that follows the actual exam. You can use this to check your progress towards being ready for the test.

Finally, a **checklist** summarises the key points covered in the unit.

Other features

Exam information boxes in each unit provide key background information about the IELTS Reading exam.

Exam tip boxes provide essential exam techniques and strategies.

Watch out! boxes highlight common errors in the exam.

Study tips

- Each unit contains approximately three hours of study material.
- Try to answer the questions without looking at a dictionary to develop the skill of guessing the meaning of unknown words from context. This is important because dictionaries cannot be used during the actual exam.
- Use a pencil to complete the exercises, so that you can erase your first answers and do the exercises again for revision.
- Try to revise what you have learnt in Parts 1 and 2 before doing the practice IELTS questions in Part 3. This will improve the quality of your answers, and using the new language will help you to remember it.
- It's recommended that you try and complete all questions in the unit as the skills needed to do well at the IELTS test can only be improved through extensive practice.
- Read the answer key carefully as this provides information on what kind of answer is awarded high marks.
- In Part 3 you are given the opportunity to put the strategies that you have learnt in Part 2 into practice. Remember to read the question carefully and complete the task in the exact way you have been asked. Do not assume that you know a particular task because you have practised similar ones in the past. There may be slight variations in the tasks in the actual IELTS test.

Other resources

Also available in the *Collins Get Ready for IELTS* series are: *Writing*, *Listening* and *Speaking*.

Free Teacher's Notes for all units are available online at: www.collinselt.com/teachielts

The International English Language Testing System (IELTS) Test

IELTS is jointly managed by the British Council, Cambridge ESOL Examinations and IDP Education, Australia.

There are two versions of the test:

- Academic
- General Training

Academic is for students wishing to study at undergraduate or postgraduate levels in an English-medium environment.

General Training is for people who wish to migrate to an English-speaking country.

This book is primarily for students taking the Academic version.

The Test

There are four modules:

Listening	30 minutes, plus 10 minutes for transferring answers to the answer sheet NB: the audio is heard *only once*. Approx. 10 questions per section Section 1: two speakers discuss a social situation Section 2: one speaker talks about a non-academic topic Section 3: up to four speakers discuss an educational project Section 4: one speaker gives a talk of general academic interest
Reading	60 minutes 3 texts, taken from authentic sources, on general, academic topics. They may contain diagrams, charts, etc. 40 questions: may include multiple choice, sentence completion, completing a diagram, graph or chart, choosing headings, yes/no, true/false questions, classification and matching exercises.
Writing	Task 1: 20 minutes: description of a table, chart, graph or diagram (150 words minimum) Task 2: 40 minutes: an essay in response to an argument or problem (250 words minimum)
Speaking	11–14 minutes A three-part face-to-face oral interview with an examiner. The interview is recorded. Part 1: introductions and general questions (4–5 mins) Part 2: individual long turn (3–4 mins) – the candidate is given a task, has one minute to prepare, then talks for 1–2 minutes, with some questions from the examiner. Part 3: two-way discussion (4–5 mins): the examiner asks further questions on the topic from Part 2, and gives the candidate the opportunity to discuss more abstract issues or ideas.
Timetabling	Listening, Reading and Writing must be taken on the same day, and in the order listed above. Speaking can be taken up to 7 days before or after the other modules.
Scoring	Each section is given a band score. The average of the four scores produces the Overall Band Score. You do not pass or fail IELTS; you receive a score.

IELTS and the Common European Framework of Reference

The CEFR shows the level of the learner and is used for many English as a Foreign Language examinations.
The table below shows the approximate CEFR level and the equivalent IELTS Overall Band Score:

CEFR description	CEFR code	IELTS Band Score
Proficient user (Advanced)	C2 C1	9 7–8
Independent user (Intermediate – Upper Intermediate)	B2 B1	5–6.5 4–5

This table contains the general descriptors for the band scores 1–9:

IELTS Band Scores		
9	Expert user	Has fully operational command of the language: appropriate, accurate and fluent with complete understanding.
8	Very good user	Has fully operational command of the language, with only occasional unsystematic inaccuracies and inappropriacies. Misunderstandings may occur in unfamiliar situations. Handles complex detailed argumentation well.
7	Good user	Has operational command of the language, though with occasional inaccuracies, inappropriacies and misunderstandings in some situations. Generally handles complex language well and understands detailed reasoning.
6	Competent user	Has generally effective command of the language despite some inaccuracies, inappropriacies and misunderstandings. Can use and understand fairly complex language, particularly in familiar situations.
5	Modest user	Has partial command of the language, coping with overall meaning in most situations, though is likely to make many mistakes. Should be able to handle basic communication in own field.
4	Limited user	Basic competence is limited to familiar situations. Has frequent problems in understanding and expression. Is not able to use complex language.
3	Extremely limited user	Conveys and understands only general meaning in very familiar situations. Frequent breakdowns in communication occur.
2	Intermittent user	No real communication is possible except for the most basic information using isolated words or short formulae in familiar situations and to meet immediate needs. Has great difficulty understanding spoken and written English.
1	Non user	Essentially has no ability to use the language beyond possibly a few isolated words.
0	Did not attempt the test	No assessable information provided.

Marking

The Listening and Reading papers have 40 items, each worth one mark if correctly answered. Here are some examples of how marks are translated into band scores:

Listening: 16 out of 40 correct answers: band score 5
23 out of 40 correct answers: band score 6
30 out of 40 correct answers: band score 7

Reading 15 out of 40 correct answers: band score 5
23 out of 40 correct answers: band score 6
30 out of 40 correct answers: band score 7

Writing and Speaking are marked according to performance descriptors.

Writing: examiners award a band score for each of four areas with equal weighting:

- Task achievement (Task 1)
- Task response (Task 2)
- Coherence and cohesion
- Lexical resource and grammatical range and accuracy

Speaking: examiners award a band score for each of four areas with equal weighting:

- Fluency and coherence
- Lexical resource
- Grammatical range
- Accuracy and pronunciation

For full details of how the examination is scored and marked, go to: www.ielts.org

1 Friendship

Part 1: Vocabulary

1   2   3   4

1a   **What do we need friends for? Match the words to the pictures. The first one has been done for you.**

> sharing   chatting   having fun   partying

1 ....*partying*......   3 ....*having fun*....

2 ...*sharing*........   4 ....*chatting*.....

1b   **Words ending in -ing are often at the beginning and at the end of sentences.**

Put the four words from exercise 1a in the correct sentences.

1   It is difficult for young children, but they have to learn that friendship is about
....*sharing*............ .

2   ....*Parting*.............. with friends is not something I do very often, but we always
celebrate our birthdays.

3   ......*Chatting*.......... with friends is one of my favourite ways to spend an afternoon.
We have so much to say that we often talk for hours.

4   Even on bad days, being with my best friend means ....*having fun*........... .

Watch Out!

Although some verbs have very similar meanings, they are not always interchangeable;
it depends on the context. For example, we *spend time* with friends, or more formally,
we *socialize* with them; more informally; we *hang out* with them. If we participate in a
specific activity, such as a game or a sport, *play* is correct e.g. *playing chess*.

2 **Which nouns go with which verbs? Copy and complete the table. Then answer the questions below.**

> chess basketball board games sports swimming tennis cards dancing
> weightlifting skiing yoga shopping exercise karate poker puzzles kick boxing hiking

Play	Go	Do
basketball chess لعبة board games Poker tennis puzzles cards Sport	swimming dancing shopping skiing hiking	sports weightlifting Puzztes yoga exercise karate kick boxing

1 Which verb do you use most with activities ending in –ing?   « go »
2 Which verb do you use most for competitive games?   « Play »
3 Which verb do you use most for other recreational activities?   « do »

3a **Read about how these people have fun. Underline all the words that refer to activities, and circle the words that refer to places. Don't use a dictionary yet.**

Jack, 15:
I spend time with my family most evenings. At the weekend, I prefer to hang out with my friends at the park or in the playground in the local woods. If it rains, I like to go to see a film with my friends.

Monica, 18:
I belong to a chess club which meets twice a month, and once a year we go camping. It's the highlight of my summer! We stay in tents on a lovely camp site and have picnics and barbecues. In the evenings, we organize quizzes and play cards. And we also play a lot of chess, of course!

Amrita, 12:
My older sisters spend a lot of time with their friends in the local shopping centre, but I'm not allowed to go out without an adult yet. I can still chat to my friends all the time though, by phone, email or text message.

3b **Find words in the texts above that match with these meanings.**

1 local shopping center: a large place where you can buy many different things
2 Monica: a person who is no longer a child
3 Camp site: a place where you can stay in a caravan or a tent
4 Picnics: a meal in the open air
5 barbecue: outdoor parties where people cook and eat food
6 Quizzes: games in which you have to answer questions

Exam information | Multiple-choice questions

In the exam, there are different types of multiple-choice questions: you may be asked to choose the correct answer to a question, or you may be given a choice of sentence endings and asked to form a sentence that reflects the meaning of the text. The questions will be in the same order as the information in the text.

1 Read the following text and then look at the questions on the next page.

The value of friendship

Recent research into the world of teenagers has suggested that they value friendship above everything else. Children aged between 12 and 15 were asked what was important to them. Their answers included possessions such as money and computer gadgets but also relationships with people. The teenagers questioned said that friends were the most important to them, more even than family, or boyfriends and girlfriends.

We wanted to find out more about the results of this research so we asked our readers what they thought about the value of friendship. Here are some examples of what they said about their friends:

Ben, 15:

Every time I have a fight with my parents, I need some time on my own. But after that, the first thing I do is meet up with my friends. After playing football for a while, or skateboarding, I usually feel much happier again.

Rory, 13:

When I moved to a village in the countryside, I thought that it would be the end of my friendships. But my old friends have kept in touch and they come and visit in the holidays. There's a lake nearby, so we often go sailing, water-skiing or windsurfing. And I have made some new friends here too, at school, and since I joined the rugby club.

Carlos, 11:

Last year, I broke my arm on a skiing holiday. Unfortunately, it was my left arm and I am left-handed. My school friends all helped and copied their notes for me.

It seems that our readers value their friendships very highly. From what they told us, they spend a lot of time with their friends, just hanging out, or sharing hobbies and interests. They seem to need their friends for advice, help, chats, and for having fun. Clearly, friends make each other feel better. Looking at what our readers told us, the results of the recent research are not really surprising.

2 Try to answer this question yourself first, before reading the explanation. Choose the best answer from the letters a–d.

To teenagers, money is …

   a not important.

   b as important as computer gadgets.

   c as important as relationships with people.

   d less important than friendships.

The correct answer is d. The teenagers said that money, gadgets and relationships are all important to them. However, the text also tells us that the teenagers value friendships most, therefore money is less important.

> ## Exam tip
>
> Deciding which are the key, or most important, words in a question can help you to locate the appropriate section of the text more quickly.

3 Look at the questions in Exercise 4, without reading the answer options. Underline the question words (e.g. *where, when, what*) and the key words in each of the questions (1–3) and sentence stems (4–5).

4 Now answer these multiple-choice questions. Choose the appropriate letter a, b, c or d.

  i   *Why are Ben, Rory and Carlos mentioned in the article?*

    a They know why teenagers value friendship.

    b They gave information about themselves.

    c They read magazines.

    d They are teenage boys.

  ii   *Which of the following best describes Ben?*

    a He often has fights.

    b He likes being alone.

    c He is happier than his friends.

    d He likes some sports.

  iii   *What do we know about the lake that Rory visits?*

    a It is near the school.

    b It is near his home.

    c It is used by a lot of people who do water sports.

    d It is in a village.

  iv   *Carlos mentions that he is left-handed because …*

    a it makes skiing harder.

    b it makes it worse that he broke the arm he uses most.

    c it is an interesting fact about himself and he was talking about his left arm.

    d it is very unfortunate when you break your left arm.

  v   *The answers to the recent research and the answers from the readers …*

    a were surprising.

    b were the same.

    c were similar.

    d were both about sports.

Friendship   **11**

Exam tip

If a question is difficult, don't spend too much time on it – go to the next one. Once you find the next answer, you can go back in the text to find the answer to the previous question. This is because, in this type of task, the questions are in the same order as the information in the text.

Questions 1–6

Choose the appropriate letters a, b, c or d.

i   How many friends do the majority of people probably have?

   a 30 real friends or fewer
   b a minimum of 30 real friends

   c 150 internet friends
   d 400 internet friends over the course of their lives

ii   It is difficult ...

   a to believe the numbers about friendship.
   b to keep your friends happy.

   c to trust what you read on social networking sites.
   d to give a definition of 'friendship'.

iii   Friendship means ...

   a different things to different people.
   b dying for your friends if you need to.

   c helping each other until it is no longer necessary.
   d accepting people with different views.

iv   Sometimes people worry because ...

   a they think that they have too many friends.
   b they spend too much time with friends.

   c they think they are too old to make friends.
   d there are no guidelines about friendship.

v   Most of us ...

   a are dissatisfied with our friends.
   b build friendships late in life.

   c are frightened to talk to strangers.
   d need to be with others.

vi   What does 'Strangers are friends we have not met yet' mean?

   a We have not met strangers before.
   b Strangers are also our friends.

   c We should not talk to strangers.
   d Strangers may become our friends.

It is said that most people have no more than 30 friends at any given time, and 400 over the whole of their lives. However, on social networking sites, most users have about 150 friends. If these numbers are correct, then friendship means different things in different situations.

majority

One of the reasons for having more online friends than real friends at a certain point in time is that online friendships do not require much time and energy: it is easy to accept friendships and keep them forever. Another possibility is that it is difficult to say 'no' when somebody asks us to be their friend online, even if we feel we don't really know them. The fact that they ask us suggests that they do consider us a friend, which is a nice feeling. Alternatively, they may be 'collectors' of online friends and just want to use us to get a higher number of friends and appear to be popular.

Online friendships are quite easy, but in the real world decisions about friendships are harder to make. There are no rules about friendship. There are no guidelines about how to make friends, how to keep friendships going, and how to finish friendships if we want to move on. People have very different opinions about this: some people would die for their friends and they value them more than family. Others say that friends are temporary, only there to help each other until they are no longer needed. If people with such different views become friends, this can lead to problems.

Because of these different definitions of friendship, it is easy to be unhappy about our friendships. We may want them to be deeper or closer, or we may want to have more friends in our lives. Sometimes we simply do not have the time to develop our friendships, or we fear we have left it too late in life to start. If we move to another country or city, we have to find ways to make new friends again.

This dissatisfaction shows us how important friendships are for most of us. We should not think that it could be too late to build friendships. We also need to understand that the need to be around other people is one that is shared by many. Therefore, we should not be too frightened about starting to talk to people who in the future may become our friends: it is likely that they too would like to get closer to us. Remember what people say: strangers are friends we have not met yet.

Progress check

How many boxes can you tick? You should work towards being able to tick them all.

Did you ...
remember to underline the key words in the questions and look for them in the text? ☐
read only the parts of the text that you needed to? ☐
remember that the questions are in the same order as the information in the text? ☐
first skip a difficult question and then go back to it after you found the answer to the next one? ☐
base your answers on the text, not on your own opinion? ☐

2 Body and mind

Part 1: Vocabulary

1a Match the following sports equipment to the pictures. Write the words.

bat   racket   board   club

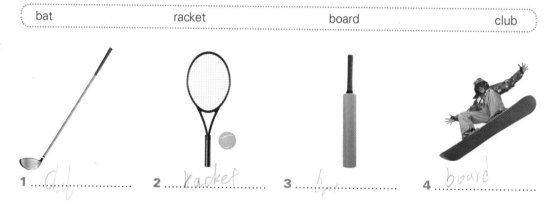

1 ....*club*.......   2 ....*racket*.......   3 ....*bat*.......   4 ....*board*.......

1b Can you name three sports that use boards?

Snow boarding   *skate boarding*   ....

1c Read the definitions. Which games and sports are being described? Choose from the box.

cricket   water polo   windsurfing   basketball   golf   netball   tennis   badminton   swimming

1 a game in which a person uses long sticks (called clubs) to hit a small, hard ball into holes that are spread out over a large area of grassy land: *golf*................

2 a game played by two or four players in which the players use a light racket to hit a cone with feathered flights (called a shuttlecock) over a high net: *badminton*......

3 a sport in which a person moves along the surface of the sea or a lake on a long narrow board with a sail on it: *windsurfing*..

4 an outdoor game played between two teams in which players try to score points (called runs), by hitting a ball with a wooden bat: *basketball*......

2 The words below describe feelings. Are they positive or negative feelings? Copy and write the words in the right categories. Use a dictionary if necessary.

afraid amazed amused angry annoyed anxious ashamed bored calm confident
curious delighted depressed disappointed embarrassed excited frightened glad
guilty happy jealous miserable nervous relaxed sad terrible tired wonderful

Pleasant / Positive feelings	Unpleasant / Negative feelings
amazed calm Confident Carious	afraid bored angry annoyed bored anxious ashamed

Watch out! *I m Portant*

A common mistake is to mix up *boring* with *bored*, or *amused* with *amusing*. The *-ed*
ending normally describes feelings, and the *-ing* ending describes things (often the cause
of the feelings).   *excited   intresting*
✗ The film was long and I was boring.   *exciting   intrested*
✓ The film was long and it was boring. / The film was long and I was bored.

3 Complete the sentences using words ending in *-ed* or *-ing*. Use a form of the verbs in the box
and try to make the sentences true for you. You can use the verbs more than once.

surprise	frighten	excite	embarrass	satisfy	annoy
disappoint	depress	amaze	tire	amuse	relax

1 In the evening I feel more ....tired.... *disappointed* than in the morning.
2 I usually find black and white films ...frightening.. *amazing*.
3 I have never found any of my exam results ..embarrassing....
4 Classical music makes me feel ~~surprised~~ *excited , relaxed*
5 There are still a lot of poor people in the world, which is ..disappointing *Pepressing*.
6 I don't have any ..exciting.. *amazing* .....hobbies.
7 I think animals are...frightening, amusing
8 I don't get easily ...annoying.., ...amused.

Exam information | Short-answer questions

In the exam, you may have to look for facts in a passage and give short answers to questions. You will be told how many words you are allowed to use in the answers. A number can be written either as a word, e.g. *four*, or as a number, e.g. *4*, and counts as one word. A word with a hyphen in it, e.g. *mother-in-law*, counts as one word. You will not be required to use contractions.

1 **How many words are there in these sentences?**

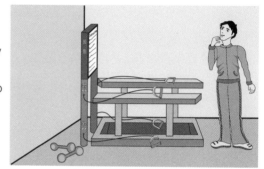

9 **1** She keeps fit by running after her two (five-year-olds.) *one word*

∞ **2** To use the gym equipment safely, follow the (step-by-step) instructions.

11 **3** The Internet is helping the (over-sixties) to find (up-to-date) health information.

13 **4** They are offering exercise classes 3 mornings a week for the (part-time) workers.

Exam tip

To keep to the maximum number of words, it can help to change a word form. Use a noun as an adjective *the documents about the house → the house documents*, or to omit a verb *there is a variety of reasons → various reasons*.

2 **The following instructions were given in an IELTS reading exam: 'Using NO MORE THAN FOUR WORDS for each, answer the following questions'.**

Look at the students' answers in the table below and make them shorter if necessary.

	Question	Students' answers	Short answer
1	What were his parents afraid of?	there was a possibility that he would have problems with his health (12 words)	*his possible health problems* (4 words)
2	When did they first find out there was a problem?	when doctors did a medical examination during the mother's pregnancy	
3	How does his illness affect him?	at the moment he is not affected by it at all but he needs to take medication	
4	What will happen in the future?	nobody knows that yet	

3 Answer these questions in NO MORE THAN THREE WORDS.

 1 What do you think is the best way to lose weight? ....
 2 How do you feel about football? ....
 3 What do you enjoy doing in your free time? ....
 4 Why is exercise important? ....

4 Read this list and cross out two activities that would <u>not</u> help you to answer the questions below.

> • reading the questions slowly before reading the text
>
> • underlining the key words in the questions
>
> ✓ reading the text before reading the questions
>
> • underlining the key words in the text
>
> • scanning (moving your eyes down over the text to find information you are looking for, without reading the text word for word)

 1 Why do some people accept pain as a part of life?
 2 What did Blaxter want to find out about?
 3 What does the text say about how older people define health?

5 Underline the key words in questions 1–3 above.

6 Now scan the text below and answer questions 1–3, using NO MORE THAN THREE WORDS for each answer.

They are older

 1 ~~age differens~~
 2 ~~define~~ health definitions
 3 able to cope

> Illness is defined in a variety of ways, which depend on a number of factors. One of these factors is age differences. Older people tend to accept as 'normal' a range of pains and physical limitations which younger people would define as symptoms of some illness or disability. As we age, we gradually redefine health and accept greater levels of physical discomfort. In Blaxter's (1990) national survey of health definitions, she found that young people tend to define health in terms of physical fitness, but gradually, as people age, health comes to be defined more in terms of being able to cope with everyday tasks. She found examples of older people with really serious arthritis, who nevertheless defined themselves as healthy, as they were still able to carry out a limited range of routine activities.

Glossary

arthritis: a medical condition in which the joints (such as the knee or fingers) in someone's body are painful

Exam information | Short-answer questions

Just as with multiple-choice questions, short-answer questions are normally in the same order as the information in the text. Sometimes in short-answer tasks, the instructions will ask you to use words taken directly from the text.

Questions 1–10

Using NO MORE THAN FOUR WORDS for each, answer the following questions.

i   In what ways do our bodies physically differ?
shapes , heights , abilities , colours.

ii   Why do our bodies differ physically?
indicates , social aging

iii   What types of jobs are poor people likely to have?
difficult , opposite , boring . inactive.

iv   What aspects of poor people's living environments are not good?
housing condition , neighbourhoods.

v   What influences how groups of people value bodies?
....

vi   What have wealthy cultures changed their opinion about?
Valuations of body shapes.

vii   In the past, what part of the body could indicate that people were rich?
....

viii   According to sociology, in what ways should we think about the body?
biological terms   social terms

ix   Which two physical factors contribute to whether people are obese or not?
....

x   What does society say that being obese is? very fat
....

The body

The concept of 'the body' is closely related to the ideas of 'illness' and 'health'.

All of us exist in 'bodies' of different shapes, heights, colours and physical abilities. The main reasons for the differences are genetic, and the fact that people's bodies change as they age. However, a huge range of research indicates that there are social factors too.

aging

junk foods

Poorer people are more likely to eat 'unhealthy' foods, to smoke cigarettes and to be employed in repetitive, physically difficult work or the opposite: boring, inactive employment. Moreover, their housing conditions and neighbourhoods tend to be worse. All of these factors impact upon the condition of a person's health: the physical shapes of bodies are strongly influenced by social factors.

These social factors are also closely linked to emotional wellbeing. People with low or no incomes are more likely to have mental health problems. It is not clear, however, whether poverty causes mental illness, or whether it is the other way around. For example, certain people with mental health issues may be at risk of becoming homeless, just as a person who is homeless may have an increased risk of illnesses such as depression.

There are other types of social factors too. Bodies are young or old, short or tall, big or small, weak or strong. Whether these judgments matter and whether they are positive or negative depends on the cultural and historical context. The culture – and media – of different societies promote very different valuations of body shapes. What is considered as attractive or ugly, normal or abnormal varies enormously. Currently, for example, in rich societies the idea of slimness is highly valued,

but historically this was different. In most societies the ideal body shape for a woman was a 'full figure' with a noticeable belly, while in middle-aged men, a large stomach indicated that they were financially successful in life. In many traditional African and Pacific island cultures, for example, a large body shape was a sign of success and a shape to be aimed at.

It is easy for people to feel undervalued because of factors they have no power to change, for example, their age and height. Equally, they can feel pressured into making changes to their appearance when there is a choice, which in extreme cases can lead to obsessions with weight loss and fitness regimes.

Sociologists, then, are suggesting that we should not just view bodies and minds in biological terms, but also in social terms. The physical body and what we seek to do with it change over time and society. This has important implications for medicine and ideas of health. Thus, the idea of people being 'obese' is physically related to large amounts of processed food, together with lack of exercise, and is therefore a medical issue. However, it has also become a mental health issue and social problem as a result of people coming to define this particular body shape as 'wrong' and unhealthy.

Progress check

How many boxes can you tick? You should work towards being able to tick them all.

Did you …

remember that the questions are in the same order as the information in the text? ☐

read the questions slowly before reading the text? ☐

use the key words technique? ☐

read the instructions carefully to know what the word limit was? ☐

count the words in your answers? ☐

check if you needed to use words from the text or not? ☐

3 Studying abroad

Part 1: Vocabulary

1a Match the following school subjects to the definitions

1 numeracy   **a** a lesson in which pupils do physical exercise or sport

2 literacy   **b** a school subject in which children learn about religion and other social matters

3 PE   **c** the ability to work with numbers and do calculations (+, −, x, /)

4 RE   **d** the ability to read and write

1b Without looking back at exercise 1, write the correct school subject below each picture.

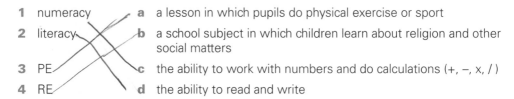

1 ....RE....   2 ..numeracy..   3 ....PE....   4 ..literacy..

2 Put the following in order, according to level of education. Rank them from low to high.

6ᵗʰ form college   nursery school   infant school   master's degree
PhD   secondary school   bachelor's degree   primary school

8 ....

7 m..

6 bachelor's degree..........

5 6th form college..........

4 secondary school..........

3 primary school..........

2 infant school..........

1 nursery school..........

3 What do you know about these student destinations and places of origin? Fill in the gaps in the table with words from the list:

> Arab   Arabic   Brussels   Dutch (x2)   German (x2)   Hanoi
> Heidelberg   Japan   Jeddah   Kyoto   Maastricht   Vietnam   Zurich

Country	Main languages	Adjective	City with one or more universities
(1) *Vietnam*	Vietnamese	Vietnamese	(2) *Hanoi* Ho Chi Minh City
(3) *Japan*	Japanese	Japanese	Tokyo (4) *Kyoto*
Saudi Arabia	(5) *Arabic*	(6) *Arab*	Riyadh (7) *Jeddah*
Germany	(8) *German*	German	(9) .... Munich
The Netherlands	(10) *Maastricht*	Dutch	Amsterdam (11) ....
Belgium	(12) .... French	Belgian	Louvain (13) ....
Switzerland	French, Italian (14)	Swiss	Geneva (15) ....

Watch Out!

'Remember' has two main uses: (1) to recall people or events from the past, e.g. *I remember how she looked that day;* (2) to retain an idea or intention in your mind, e.g. *He didn't remember to call me.*

If you help someone else to remember something, you *remind* them about it:

✗ Can you remember me to take a coat?   ✓ Can you remind me to take a coat?

4 Complete these sentences with *remember* or *remind*.

1 Goodbye. I will always .... you.

2 Hello again. Do you .... me?

3 She always .... him that he needs to take his medicine.

4 Do you always .... to take your medicine?

5 .... me to take my medicine.

Exam information | Completing tables and flow charts

In the exam, you may be given a table or a flow chart (a series of steps linked by arrows) with gaps in it. You will need to read a passage to find the missing information. The answers may be in one particular section of the text, but are unlikely to be in the same order as the gaps.

You will be told how many words from the text you should use, e.g. *no more than two words and/or a number, one word only.*

Exam tip

Scanning is a very useful technique, because it saves time. It means that you move your eyes down the text quickly to find specific information, e.g. places, names, phrases, without reading everything properly and ignoring information you do not need.

The following four exercises help you practise scanning. They all refer to the text opposite.

1 Use the organization of the text to help you. Look at the text quickly to decide which paragraph(s) you would need to read properly if you only wanted to find out about the reasons why people choose to study abroad.

Paragraph number(s): ....

2 Scan the text to find names of countries, people and organizations. Copy and complete the table.

Countries	People	Organizations or institutions
UK, US, Malaysia, Japan, Germany	Russell	British Council

Exam tip

Use the text style or formatting to help you find the areas in the text that you are looking for, e.g. uppercase letters, numbers, italics, bold print, quotation marks and other visual information. ABCDE   AB   « »

3 Do this exercise in less than one minute if you can. First copy the table in your notebook. Then scan the text for the different items. Check in the Answer key to see if you found them all within the time limit.

numbers	5, 11, 10, 1
words in italics	needed, internationalization
words in bold print	
abbreviations	

US, UK, UAE.

بروتوسیت ایک

4 Scan the text quickly to answer the following questions.

    1 Which paragraph(s) give(s) somebody's opinion?

    2 What does somebody really want people to understand?

    3 Which two paragraphs talk about the country that is the most welcoming to overseas students?

    4 Which paragraph gives examples to explain what an internationalization approach is?

5 How did you find the answers without reading properly?

Is it better to go abroad to study?

Student-friendly places

The British Council has named the universities that are most welcoming to overseas students. As you would expect, English-speaking countries such as Australia, the UK and the US have made the top 10, but the number one may be a surprise: Germany. Two Far Eastern countries, i.e. China and Malaysia, made it to the top 5, ranking higher than the US, Japan, Russia, Nigeria and Brazil.

The benefits of studying abroad

Russell Howe, a Scot who is currently studying a Business degree at Stellinga International College in the Netherlands, previously also studied in India (which came 11th on the list). 'People often ask me why I needed to travel, because British universities have a good reputation elsewhere in the world. But this is not something I needed to do, but something I really wanted to do. I have learnt different ways of looking at things, but I also found out how much we all have in common, wherever we are from. All of this will be useful in my future career.'

Russell is not the only international student in his department. Business and administrative courses are the most popular with international students, followed by engineering and technology, social studies, creative arts and design, medicine-related topics and law. Manal, a student at the Faculty of Art and Design at Stellinga, says she has similar reasons to Russell, but there is more: 'I wanted to broaden my understanding of the world. I have enhanced my language skills: I am more fluent in English and have also taken a level 1 Dutch evening class. One of my modules is about European art, and I believe that I am benefiting more from studying this in Europe than anywhere else. I have managed to visit other countries in my holidays, and really feel that this whole experience is developing my global perspective. I also hope that I have made lasting friendships and contacts.'

Enabling student access

What is it that makes these countries student-friendly? Well, all of them make it easy for international students to apply, and provide ongoing support once they are there. They also offer good quality degrees, which are valued highly in other countries too. The fact that Germany came out as winner is probably due to the country's efforts towards internationalization. One aspect of this is that the country welcomes foreign students by charging them the same fees as home students, meaning that in some universities overseas students study for free. Many classes are conducted in English, and so are most leaflets, making it easier for international students to keep informed and take part in student life.

Apart from the financial reasons already mentioned, this type of educational internationalization can help with the quality of research in these universities, through e.g. networking, team work and the sharing of skills. For students, it is a valuable addition to their skills and experience at a time when jobs are not easy to find.

Glossary

British Council: an organization that connects people worldwide with learning opportunities and creative ideas from the UK.

Questions 1–11

Using NO MORE THAN TWO WORDS from the passage for each answer, complete the table and the flow chart below.

The required documents:

Evidence of language ability	IELTS 6.5 or (1) *equivalent*
Evidence of studies	(2) *International Baccalaureate* Dutch VWO diploma, or other secondary school diploma
Information about motivation	(3) *Personal statement* with a maximum length of (4) *1000 words*
Proof of identity	(5) *Passport* and passport photo
Other	(6) *translations* if originals are in a foreign language

The online application process for people outside the EU:

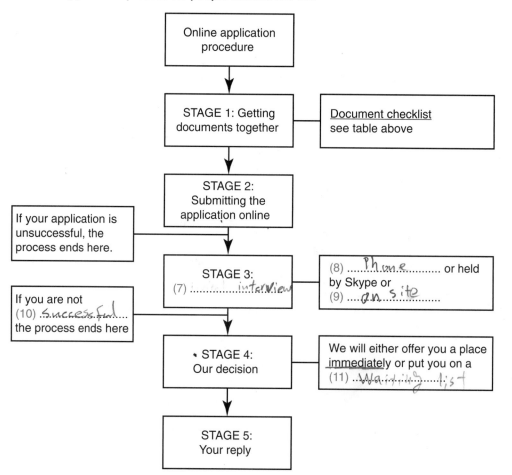

Applying to Stellinga College

Why Stellinga?

Thank you for your interest in Stellinga International College. As an international student, we are sure you will find our university college an exciting place to study, with like-minded and ambitious individuals.

Preparing and submitting your application

We have tried to make the application process as easy as possible for you, but there are a number of procedures you must follow.

All our courses are taught in English, so first of all you will probably need to submit proof of your English language ability. We require an IELTS score of 6.5 or another test result which is equivalent (see appendix). You will also have to send us your secondary school diploma, so that we can evaluate it. If you have the International Baccalaureate or a Dutch VWO diploma, you don't need to provide English language test results.

We will also require a personal statement. This is a text of up to 1000 words in which you introduce yourself, explain your interest in our college, and why you want to study your chosen course.

If you are from outside the European Union (EU), it is important that you have an entrance visa before you come to study in the Netherlands, but we will apply for this for you.

We now only accept online applications, so please ensure that you have all your documents ready to upload before you begin. Any documents that are not in English originally will also need to be translated and the translations also uploaded.

You will need a passport photograph; a copy of your passport; copies of all your certificates, diplomas, etc.; your proof of language ability (see above); and your personal statement in English.

What happens next?

Your application will then be considered. If your initial application is successful, you will be invited for an interview. This will be conducted in English via Skype, over the phone or on site, depending on whether you can come and visit us. You will talk to two or three members of staff for up to 30 minutes, and will be asked to elaborate on your application documents and your personal statement. We aim to inform you of our decision in writing, within 4 weeks. There are several possible outcomes: you may not have been successful; you may be offered a place at the college or you may be offered a place on the waiting list. You will need to reply to any offers within two weeks, otherwise your place may be offered to somebody else.

Good luck with your application.

Progress check

How many boxes can you tick? You should work towards being able to tick them all.

Did you …

use scanning techniques?	☐
read thoroughly only the parts of the text that you needed to?	☐
read the instructions carefully to know what the word limit was?	☐
count the words in your answers?	☐
only use words that were in the text?	☐

Review 1

1 Answer the following questions about yourself in NO MORE THAN THREE WORDS. This may be difficult to do but it will help you practise keeping within word limits.

    1 What is your favourite meal?

    2 What did you do yesterday?

    3 What is the best thing that has happened to you in your life so far?

    4 What is the best advice you have ever been given?

    5 If you could do anything you wanted right now, what would it be?

    6 What do you dream about?

2 Match the sentence stems with the correct endings. You will not use all of the endings.

1	I don't mind spending	**a**	a campsite but I never go there.
2	I like to play	**b**	a picnic with my parents in a tent.
3	If you don't like meat, you probably won't like	**c**	a quiz at the social club, which is open to anyone.
4	I have bought	**d**	at the shopping centre.
5	I live near	**e**	that children under 14 should not be left on their own.
6	I like hanging out with my friends	**f**	money is more important than friendship.
7	Every Monday there is	**g**	tennis at the weekends.
8	I believe that	**h**	the piano from a friend.
		i	the woods in my spare time.
		j	time with my parents, but not when I am on holiday.
		k	barbecues.
		l	with my friends after college.

3 Match the verbs in the box to the words below to make correct collocations.

> keep   play   study   value   take   charge   have

1 ....*charge*.... fees

2 ....*keep*.... a class

3 ....*play*.... in touch

4 ....*have*.... fun

5 ....*take*.... friendship

6 ....*value*.... cards

7 ....*study*.... abroad

4 Correct the mistakes, if any, in the following sentences.

   1 I can't think of anything more bored than a picnic in the park.
   2 Have you reminded her that it starts at half past eight?
   3 When I have no college work, I usually go to my friends to play.
   4 Can you remember me that I need to do some washing?
   5 I have never felt so sad and depressing in my life.
   6 Party with friends is my favourite activity.
   7 I am very exciting to see you.
   8 There is no need to be embarrassed, just come in.

5 How might these people be feeling? Use words ending in *-ed.*

1 .... **2** .... **3** ....

4 .... **5** ....

6 The following words are related to the topic of education, but all the vowels have been left out. Can you put them back in?

   1 ltrc   ....
   2 nmrc   ....
   3 stdnt   ....
   4 nvrsty   ....
   5 dgr   ....
   6 rsrch   ....
   7 dplm   ....
   8 pplctn   ....

4 Science and technology at home

Part 1: Vocabulary

 **1**  **2**  **3**  **4**

1a The equipment in the pictures can all be found in the homes of many cooks. Match the words to the items.

> kitchen scales *(4)*   measuring jug *(1)*   flask *(2)*   kettle *(3)*

1 _measuring jug_   3 _kettle_
2 _flask_   4 _kitchen scales_

1b Use the words from exercise 1a to complete these sentences.

1 A _Kettle_ is probably the most used piece of kitchen equipment in many countries because most people enjoy hot drinks.

2 If you like hot food or hot drinks, it is worth buying a _Flask_ to take with you to college or work.

3 I don't use _kitchen scales_ anymore when I am making bread: I just guess the quantities that I need.

4 A _measuring jug_ is useful for holding, measuring and transferring liquids.

2a Use the information in the table to complete the matching exercise below. The first one has been done for you.

Word part	Meaning
-metre/-meter	measure, record
-logy	the science or study of

Word part	Meaning
-graphy	the writing or drawing of
bio-	life
auto-	self
thermo-	temperature
eco-	related to physical surroundings
zoo-	animal
ge(o)-	the earth or land
hydro-	water
chrono-	time

1 barometer   **a** an extremely accurate clock that is used especially by sailors at sea

2 chronometer   **b** the study of the relationships between plants, animals, people and their environment, and the balances between these relationships

3 thermometer   **c** the study of the Earth's structure, surface and origin

4 ecology   **d** the study of the countries of the world and of such things as the land, seas, climate, towns and population

5 biology   **e** the scientific study of animals

6 geology   **f** the science related to the study of living things

7 zoology   **g** an instrument that measures air pressure and shows when the weather is changing

8 hydrology   **h** an instrument for measuring temperature, usually consisting of a narrow glass tube containing a thin column of a liquid which rises and falls as the temperature rises and falls

9 geography   **i** the study and recording (mapping) of the oceans, seas and rivers

10 hydrography   **j** the study of the distribution, conservation, use, etc. of the water of the Earth and its atmosphere

2b **Use the above information to complete the definitions for the following words.**

1 *a biography:* .... a book .... about another person's .... life ....

2 *an autobiography:* a book ....

Watch Out!

Knowing the meaning of word parts can often help you work out the overall meaning, but there are words where this does not work. For example, *dis-* often means 'opposite', *advantage / disadvantage; agree / disagree; appear / disappear; connect / disconnect; honest / dishonest*, but sometimes *dis* is not a separate word part or does not have that meaning, as in *disaster, discuss.*

Exam information | Completing sentences

In the exam, you may be asked to complete sentences with words from the passage.
The information will be in the same order as the questions.

Exam tip

The sentences will refer to information in the text, but this will be paraphrased and will
include synonyms (words or expressions that mean the same) and antonyms (words or
expressions that mean the opposite). You should scan the text to look for paraphrases of
the sentences to find the section and information you need.

1 **Match the words with their (near) synonyms.**

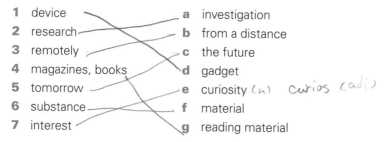

1	device	a	investigation
2	research	b	from a distance
3	remotely	c	the future
4	magazines, books	d	gadget
5	tomorrow	e	curiosity (n) curios (adj)
6	substance	f	material
7	interest	g	reading material

2 **Match the words with their (near) antonyms**

1	digital	a	the future
2	yesterday	b	deliberate
3	remote	c	commemorated
4	forgotten	d	analogue
5	lost	e	nearby
6	accidental	f	found

3 **In the following sentences, underline any words that refer to a similar idea or thing. The first
one has been done for you.**

1 Your mobile phone contains small amounts of <u>gold and platinum</u>, as well as less
<u>valuable metals</u>.
2 There are some <u>materials that allow electricity to pass through them</u>. These <u>electrical
conductors</u> are used in many different appliances in the home.
3 Another example is <u>electrical insulators</u>, substances that <u>do not let electricity pass through</u>.
4 We sell any <u>computer</u> you can imagine, from the traditional desktop to tablet
computers and other kinds of mobile <u>computers</u>, as well as cameras and e-readers.
5 Your smartphone's <u>operating system</u> may have the same or a different <u>OS</u> to the one
controlling your tablet.

Exam tip

Timing is very important in the IELTS exam, as you will have to answer 40 questions about three reading passages in one hour. In this type of exam question, you will be looking for detailed information, so you will need to use your scanning skills. Try to get used to scanning and working as fast as you can.

4 Scan the text below for the following words, or their (near) synonyms. Try to find them all, or as many as you can, in less than 90 seconds. They are in the same order.

1 parts	**6** a very large amount	**11** transfer
2 typical	**7** coat (verb)	**12** surround
3 crystal	**8** exceptional	**13** following
4 include	**9** corrode	**14** material
5 circuits	**10** tiny	**15** folded

Mobile phone components

An average basic mobile phone contains a circuit board, an antenna, a liquid crystal display, a keyboard, a microphone, a speaker and a battery.

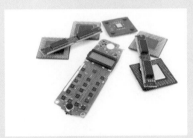

Mobile metals

Mobiles contain many different metals:

- Copper is used for electrical circuits because it is a good electrical conductor.

- Silver is used in switches on the circuit boards and in the phone buttons because it is an even better electrical conductor. It lasts for millions of on/off cycles.

- Gold is used to plate the surfaces of the circuit board and the connectors. It is an excellent electrical conductor and does not corrode.

- Tantalum is used in the electronic components. It enables scientists to make mobiles very small.

Your mobile is also likely to contain palladium, platinum, aluminium and iron.

Electrical conductivity

Metals conduct electrical currents well. Non-metals usually make good insulators. In a mobile, electrical insulators surround the circuit.

Smart mobiles

The next generation of mobile could be made from 'smart' fabric. These types of fabric react to something in the environment and change. A smart fabric mobile could be folded and put in your pocket without breaking.

Exam tip

In the exam, do not be tempted to use any previous knowledge you may have on a particular topic. You must always answer according to the information given in the text.

Questions 1–5

Complete the sentences below. Choose NO MORE THAN TWO WORDS OR NUMBERS from the text for each answer.

i A compound cannot be separated without energy and a ....*chemical reaction*....

ii Although mixtures consist of a combination of elements and compounds, it is possible for these to be ....*separated out*....

iii If flavourings were not added, people would probably ....*refuse*.... to [*car*] consume margarine.

iv Flavours can only be described as natural if they have a natural ....*sources,*....

v Vanillin is chemically produced, but ....*identical*.... in chemical composition to a natural flavouring.

Cupcakes are made from a mixture of ingredients. Different flavoured cupcakes have different mixtures. The icing used to decorate the cakes contains sugar, water, colouring and flavouring. Water and sugar are different types of compounds. These compounds are made from elements.

Elements, compounds and mixtures
Chemical substances occur in three types.

- Elements – these contain one type of atom only. They cannot be chemically broken down into simpler substances.
- Compounds – these contain two or more different elements bonded together. A chemical reaction is needed to break up a compound. This will involve energy.
- Mixtures – these may contain two or more elements and/or compounds. They are mixed in any proportion and can be separated out.

When a baker mixes the flour, sugar, fat, eggs, flavouring and colour together to make cupcakes, he or she is making a mixture. The icing sugar, water and colour make a different mixture. The sugar and water are compounds.

The compound water is made from the elements hydrogen and oxygen. Sugar contains the elements hydrogen, oxygen and carbon.

In this unit, we will be looking at flavourings, the substances that are added to food or drink to give it a particular taste. They are added because people would probably refuse to eat certain products without them. Margarine and ice cream, for example, would have unacceptable tastes, whereas certain jellies, some other sweets, and meat replacement products would have little or no taste.

Natural flavours are those found in nature. Those from vegetable sources include vanilla, strawberry, lemon and nuts. An example of an animal source is beef flavouring, added for example to chips. Essential oils and fruit juices can also be used to flavour foods. They are sourced in nature and obtained through physical processes such as distillation and fermentation.

Some animal flavours, such as bacon and beef flavour in crisps, are vegetarian because they are artificial rather than made from animal sources.

There are also nature-identical flavourings. An example is vanillin, which is often produced cheaply from lignin, a polymer, rather than from vanilla pods. These flavourings are chemically identical to natural flavourings, but have been produced chemically rather than naturally, e.g. by a process of chemical extraction. The human body does not notice the difference as their molecules are identical to natural ones.

Artificial flavourings consist of chemically synthesized compounds which have no source whatsoever in nature. Although the word natural has positive connotations, some natural flavours may have contaminated sources, which are harmful. Artificial flavours undergo strict testing because they are subject to laws (e.g. The European Flavouring Regulation (1334/2008) and may therefore be purer and safer. Using natural flavourings is also more expensive and may be considered a waste at a time when we are trying to preserve nature.

Glossary

polymer: a naturally occurring or synthetic compound

Progress check

How many boxes can you tick? You should work towards being able to tick them all.

Did you …
scan for words from the sentences or their equivalents in the text? ☐
remember that the questions are in the same order as the information in the text? ☐
skip a difficult question and then go back to it after you found the answer to the next one? ☐
base your answers on the text, not on your own guesses? ☐

5 Back to nature

AIMS: Vocabulary related to the natural world • Linking words • Skim-reading • Completing and labelling diagrams

Part 1: Vocabulary

1 _wather fall_   2 _Vally_   3 _bay_   4 _Cliff_

1 The following words refer to the natural world. Use the words to label the pictures above.

> bay   valley   cliff   waterfall

2 These words sometimes refer to similar things, but they are not interchangeable. In the sentences below, there is only one correct choice. Complete the sentences with the words in the box.

> soil   sand   land   ground

1 The house we are buying comes with a lot of ....
2 Children love playing in the ....
3 There were no chairs in the hall so we all sat on the ....
4 I have bought a big bag of .... so I can do some planting in the garden later.

3a Read the following texts, without using a dictionary. Underline all the words that refer to the natural world, and highlight all the linking words.

Our knowledge of Natural History would not be what it is today without the work of women explorers, artists and scientists. In this leaflet, you will learn about three British pioneering women, first to be involved in uncovering some of the rich history of the natural world.

Mary Anning (1799–1847)
Mary came from a poor family who lived in Lyme Regis, a coastal town in the South West of England. Her father tried to make extra money by selling fossils (remains in rocks) to rich tourists. Consequently, Mary and her

siblings learned from an early age how to look for fossils, although she was the only one of the brothers and sisters who became an expert because she understood that fossils were of interest to geology and biology, not just tourism. However, in her lifetime she did not always get the credit she deserved, as it was male geologists who published the descriptions of any finds. Her important finds include the first skeleton of an ichthyosaur, or fish-lizard, a plesiosaur, also known as sea-dragon, and a pterodactyl, a 'flying dragon'.

Collecting fossils on the cliffs was dangerous work. Mary's dog Tray was killed when rocks and earth fell down a cliff, and she nearly lost her life in the same landslide, but in the end it was cancer that killed her when she was 47.

Dorothea Bate (1878–1951)

Born in the Welsh countryside, she had a passion for outdoor pursuits and natural history from an early age. She became the first female scientist in the Natural History museum in London. She was a palaeontologist, that is, a scientist who studies fossils in order to understand the history of life on earth. She went to mountains and cliffs in the Mediterranean and explored hilltops in Bethlehem, discovering and documenting animal fossils. She wrote hundreds of reports, reviews and papers.

Evelyn Cheesman (1881–1969)

Although Evelyn wanted to become a veterinary surgeon, this was not possible for women in the early 20th century. Instead, she trained as a canine nurse. Her first job, however, was not related to dogs: she worked in the insect house at the London Zoological society. She was very adventurous and went on many expeditions to remote locations, as far away as the Galapagos Islands. Despite being very busy, she managed to publish 16 books.

3b Difficult words are often explained in texts. Find the explanations of the following words in the texts. The first one has been done for you.

| ① pioneering | ② Lyme Regis | ③ fossils | ④ siblings | ⑤ ichthyosaur | 6 plesiosaur |
| ⑦ pterodactyl | ⑧ Tray | ⑨ landslide | ⑩ palaeontologist | ⑪ canine | ⑫ remote |

pioneering – first to be involved in

Watch Out!

The exact meaning of linking words is not always clear. For example, 'in fact' is not used just to introduce *any* facts; they have to be *surprising* or *contrasting* facts (in comparison to what has just been said).

✗ Many people argue as to who is more intelligent, women or men. In fact, a study found that women scientists were more intelligent than men in similar jobs.

✓ In the past, people thought that women were less intelligent than men, because of genetic differences. In fact, according to one study, women scientists were more intelligent than men in similar jobs.

4 Do the following extracts use *in fact* correctly? Mark each extract with a ✓ or ✗.

1 It is often believed that watching a lot of TV makes people see the world as a frightening place. In fact, evidence shows that watching TV makes no difference.

2 It is often believed that watching a lot of TV makes people see the world as a frightening place. In fact, there is some evidence that this is the case.

Exam information | Completing diagram labels

In the exam, you may be asked to read a passage and use words from it to complete labels on a diagram or picture. The answers will often come from a particular section of the text and may not be in the same order as the questions.

1   **Skim-read the passage below and tick when you have found the sections that refer to:**

what jellyfish look like   1   how fossils are formed   3

what barnacles are   2   how seashells are formed   4

Part one: The beach, a natural treasure trove

Nature walks can be fun, energizing and educational at the same time. In Part One, we will look at what we can find on a marine walk. In Part Two, we will discuss our fascinating forests.

First of all, when you are walking on the beach you may be able to spot tracks. Birds and crabs leave footprints behind, especially in wet sand. On sandy beaches you will also be able to find interesting holes, made by crabs that were digging for food in the mud.

You may also come across jellyfish, as these are often washed up on the beach by the tides. They have no eyes, ears, heart or head and are mostly made of water. They look like a bag with arms, which are called tentacles. These contain poison, which helps them catch food. Even when they are out of the water or in pieces the tentacles may sting you, so they are best left alone.

Other animals you may find are coral and barnacles. The latter are marine animals that are related to crabs and lobsters and live in shallow waters. They like to attach themselves to hard materials, so you are likely to find them stuck to a piece of wood.

You may also see what look like small gelatinous blobs but are actually fish or worm eggs.

If you are lucky, you may find a fossil. In essence, this is an animal that died and got buried in a sea bed. They are likely to look like a piece of rock with an imprint of an animal skeleton. Their history is very interesting.

For an animal to become fossilized, it has to be buried in mud, sand or soil. If an animal dies but is not buried, it is more likely to rot away, be swept away by wind or water, and/or be eaten by another animal. Over millions of years, the animal remains become buried deeper and deeper; the mud, sand or soil compresses and slowly becomes rock. Their bone or shell starts to crystallize, because of surrounding minerals and chemicals. Ideally, the temperature stays relatively constant throughout this process. Sometimes the fossil dissolves completely and just leaves an imprint. At other times, waves, tides and currents slowly make the rocks erode, which allows the animal remains to break off, ready for you to find.

What you will definitely find a beach are shells. These were once the homes of animals such as snails, barnacles and mussels, consisting of a hard layer that the animal created for protection as part of its body. After the animal has died, its soft parts have rotted or have been eaten by other animals, such as crabs. What is left is a beautiful seashell for you to admire and take home if you wish.

Exam tip

In the exam, you may have to complete labels of pictures, diagrams, flow charts, etc. so it helps if you can think visually. If you do not have a visual imagination, start practising by trying to visually represent written information where possible.

2 Cover the diagrams below. Now try to make a drawing to represent the information in the paragraph about how fossils are formed.

3 Using **NO MORE THAN FOUR WORDS** from the passage, complete each gap in the diagram.

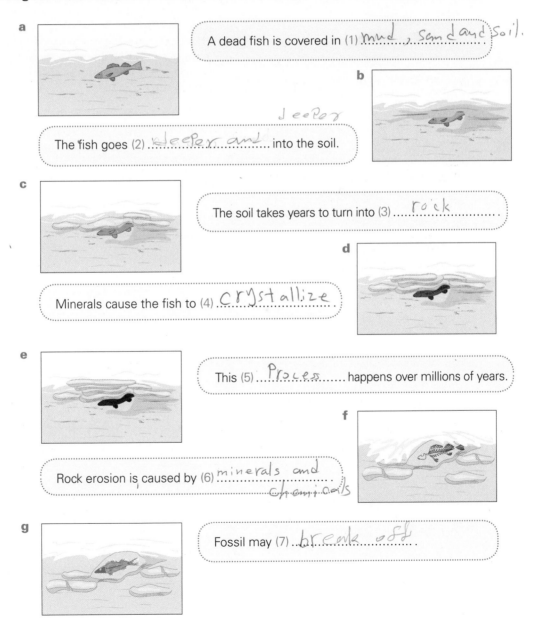

a

A dead fish is covered in (1) mud, sand and soil.

b

The fish goes (2) deeper and into the soil.

c

The soil takes years to turn into (3) rock

d

Minerals cause the fish to (4) crystallize

e

This (5) process happens over millions of years.

f

Rock erosion is caused by (6) minerals and chemicals

g

Fossil may (7) break off

Using NO MORE THAN TWO WORDS from the passage, complete each gap in the diagram.

The many uses of the Moringa tree

The Moringa tree, Saragwa, or Drumstick tree, is relatively unknown in the West, despite the fact that it is incredibly useful. Miriam Tayne reports about its culinary, medicinal and other uses.

The Moringa tree is a relatively small tree that typically grows to between three and ten metres tall. Its flowers are creamy-coloured and have been compared to small orchids. The plant has long and round green pods that can grow to 30 cms and which look a bit like drumsticks, hence the tree's common name. The pods consist of three parts, which contain round, dark brown seeds. Planting needs to be done in sandy or muddy soil, using these seeds or tree cuttings. The plant does not tolerate frost but thrives in hot climates. It is very common in South and South-east Asia, Africa and America.

The leaves are reputed to have anti-inflammatory and anti-bacterial properties, so are used for eye and ear infections, fevers, etc. They are also held against the forehead to reduce headaches, or made into tea to treat stomach complaints. As they contain a lot of iron they have been used for the treatment of anaemia, a medical condition in which there are too few red cells in the blood, causing tiredness. The plant also contains many other nutrients, such as phosphorus, calcium, potassium, and vitamins A and C.

The ground-up seeds are commonly used to treat certain skin infections, but can be used for much more. Ground seeds can be mixed with salt or oils to apply to the body to treat cramp, back ache and forms of arthritis, a medical condition in which the joints are swollen and painful. The oil, called Ben oil because it contains behenic acid, is also used as a hair treatment or a perfume, and to deter mosquitoes and treat their bites. The by-products of the oil manufacturing process are used for fertilization and water purification.

The roots work in exactly the same way as the seeds, but are much stronger, so are not used as often. They have additional uses for heart and circulation problems, whereas the gum is sometimes used to treat asthma. The bark has quite a pleasant taste and is sometimes eaten to encourage digestion.

The plant's main use is as food: for livestock, and for human beings, because it contains high concentrations of fibre and protein. The drumsticks are eaten in soup and/or as green beans, often in combination with shrimp (see picture), whereas the seeds are eaten like peas, or roasted. The leaves are eaten fresh or cooked in similar ways to spinach. Chopped, they are used as a garnish on soups and salads. They are often pickled or dried so that they are always available to use in sauces, stir-fries, soups and in sweet and sour or spicy curries.

Like every other part of the tree, its flowers are not just decorative but also functional. They taste a bit like wild mushrooms and are considered a delicacy. They are used to make tea to treat the common cold, mixed with honey to make cough medicine,  and made into juice to be drunk during breastfeeding as it is said to increase milk flow.

There is not a part of the tree that is not used. The Moringa tree is probably the most beneficial tree in the world.

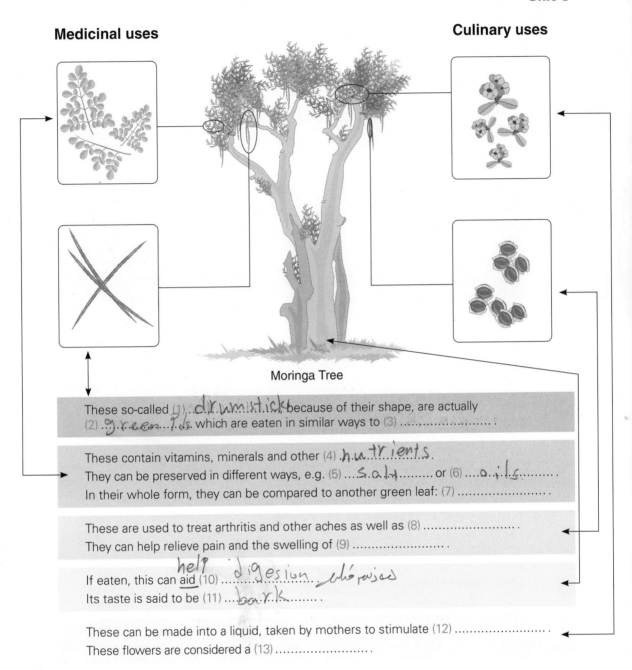

Medicinal uses

Culinary uses

Moringa Tree

These so-called (1) ...drumstick.. because of their shape, are actually
(2) ...green...?..s. which are eaten in similar ways to (3) ....

These contain vitamins, minerals and other (4) ..nutrients.
They can be preserved in different ways, e.g. (5) ....salt........ or (6) ....oils........
In their whole form, they can be compared to another green leaf: (7) ....

These are used to treat arthritis and other aches as well as (8) ....
They can help relieve pain and the swelling of (9) ....

If eaten, this can aid (10) .....help...digesion...whopajes.
Its taste is said to be (11) ...bark........ .

These can be made into a liquid, taken by mothers to stimulate (12) ....
These flowers are considered a (13) ....

Progress check

How many boxes can you tick? You should work towards being able to tick them all.

Did you...
remember to skim-read to find the right section in the text?
count your words to make sure you did not use too many?
try to visualize the information while you were reading?
look for the explanation of unknown words in the text?

6 Communication

Part 1: Vocabulary

1   When starting a company, you need to find ways of letting people know about it. What types of communication has this restaurant used? Label the pictures with the words in the box.

> slogan   advertisement   logo   sign

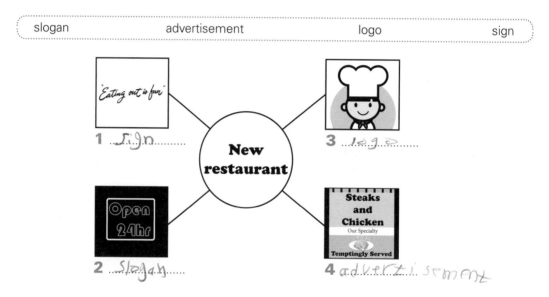

"Eating out is fun"

1 ..Sign........

New restaurant

3 ..logo....

Open 24hr

2 ..Slogan.....

Steaks and Chicken
Our Specialty
Temptingly Served

4 advertisement

2a   In the opposite text, underline the words that refer to types of messages. Don't use a dictionary. Then find words that mean:

1   ....: unwanted emails sent to a large number of people, as a way of advertising

2   ....: the practice of a company paying for its product to be placed in a clear position in a film or television programme as a form of advertising

3   ....: very large signs on which posters are displayed

4   ....: a small printed notice, usually distributed by hand, which is used to advertise a particular company, service or event

5   ....: pieces of wood that have been painted with pictures or words and which give some information about a particular place, product or event

6   ....: a person who acquires goods and services for his or her own personal needs

7   ....: a small window containing an advertisement that appears on a computer screen

It's impossible to avoid advertisements. In our homes, newspaper, magazine and television ads compete for our attention. Posters, billboards and flyers greet us the moment we walk out the door. Advertising agencies stay busy thinking up new ways to get our attention. We have company logos on our clothes. Our email is full of spam, and pop-ups slow us down as we surf the Web. Product placements sneak into films and TV shows. 'Ad wrapping' turns cars into moving signboards. Advertisers have even tried advertising in TV commercials in a subliminal way (affecting your mind without you knowing it). It's no wonder that this is called the consumer age.

2b **Find words in the above text that collocate (go together with) the words in the table.**

1	newspaper		5		logos
2		ads	6		placements
3			7		commercials
4		agencies	8		age

3a **Complete the passage with the words in the box.**

> comments   individuals   website   web   corporation   focus   activity

The word 'blog' is a combination of the words (1) '.......................' and log. It is a (2) .... containing a series of dated entries. A blog can (3) .... on a single subject of interest. Most blogs are written by (4) .... But sometimes a political committee, (5) .... or other group maintains a blog. Many blogs invite readers to leave (6) .... on the site. This often results in a community of bloggers who write back and forth to each other. The total group of web logs is the blogosphere. A 'blogstorm' occurs when there is a lot of blog (7) .... on a certain topic.

Watch out!

Articles are small words that can contain a lot of information. Look at these slogans:

> *Go to work on an egg.* (The Egg Council)
> *The ultimate driving machine.* (BMW)

The first slogan, which uses the indefinite article (a) suggests that any egg will do. The second one uses the definite article (*the*) to suggest that there is only one ultimate driving machine, a car from their specific brand.

3b **Do the following nouns relate to general or more specific information? Complete the sentences with *a(n)* or *the*.**

1 .... blog can be written by individuals or groups.
2 Within seconds of leaving your house, you will probably see .... advertisement.
3 I quite enjoy watching ....TV commercial for the first time.
4 Technology is very important in .... world of advertising.
5 Yellow is .... colour to be seen in this season.

Exam information | Completing notes and summaries

In the IELTS exam, you may be given a summary of, or notes about, a text, but there will be information missing which you will have to look for. You will usually find the information in a particular part of the text, but not in the same order. You will either have to choose words from the text or choose the correct option from those given.

Exam tip

It is often easier to choose the correct answer if you can predict the type of word you need by using your knowledge of grammar.

1 **Copy and complete the table. Some words belong in more than one category.**

satellite   mobile   newspaper   transfer   broadband   fast   consumer

access   free   speedy   handy   keyboard   signal   commercial

adjectives	nouns	verbs	adverbs

2 **Read the sentences. Predict what type of word is missing in each gap and give an example of a possible answer. The first one has been done for you.**

1 Websites allow us to .... a library's catalogue of books and periodicals.

The structure is allow somebody to do (verb) something. There are a number of possibilities, e.g. access, consult, preview, see.

2 Public libraries are changing. You can still borrow and .... books, magazines, DVDs, CDs and other media.

3 *Communication* refers to both the act of ...., in other words the exchange of information, ideas or feelings, and something that is ...., for example a letter or telephone call.

4 DVDs aren't just for films anymore. New DVDs (digital video discs) provide even .... sound quality than audio CDs (compact discs).

5 Both CDs and DVDs sample the music, but DVDs are able to .... more information and they have more samples per second. The information is also more ....

6 After 1066, many French and Latin words came .... the English language.

3 Here are some notes (a) and a summary (b) based on the text below. First, use your skim-reading and/or scanning skills to decide which sections of the text they come from. Next, look for the missing words in these sections, using your knowledge of grammar to identify them. Use no more than TWO words from the text each time.

a

> types of communication:
> (1) ....
> (2) ....written........ } verbal
> (3) ....

b

> It is important to follow the rules when communicating in writing, especially if you are in (1) .... environment. There are three areas which are important: (2) ...., content and language. The language needs to be formal and there should be no (3) .... You cannot choose to include exactly what you like, for example financial information must be included in your business's (4) .... It also needs to look good on the page, with everything written in a (5) .... format.

In all communication, whether this is verbal or non-verbal, a sender transfers a message to a receiver, choosing a certain medium. The receiver uses the message clues and the context, and decodes it to understand it. This is often followed by a new message in return, and so the communication process continues.

Although this procedure is always the same, it can take many different forms depending on the type of communication. For example, in non-verbal communication (as opposed to written and spoken communication, which are both verbal), the code used could be gestures, body language, eye contact and facial expressions, such as a smile.

Communication is extremely important in the business world. It is likely that in this context both informal and formal styles will be used. If we take the example of meetings, we might say that they are often conducted in quite a relaxed way, with participants using first names and informal language. However, as soon as the meeting is official, careful records, called minutes, will be kept, following a predetermined format which is standard across many business situations. Layout is one aspect of a formal style. Content will also be dictated to some extent by the level of formality. Annual business reports must include certain types of information to be legal, e.g. financial information, but even a simple letter would not function as it should without the use of somebody's title (e.g. *Mr* or *Ms*). Language is another aspect which needs to be taken into account. Formal, written communication needs to be clear and to the point, without spelling or grammar mistakes, and in a formal register (e.g. *Dear ...*, instead of *Hi*). Not following these important rules would have a negative effect in any business context.

> **Exam tip**
>
> Training yourself to work against the clock will help you with your timing during the exam.

1   Answer the following questions about the passage below within two minutes. Use words from the passage for your answers. Note that these questions follow the order of the information in the text and have no word limit (just for this exercise).

   i   Name a complaint that is often made about managers in the United Kingdom.
   ii   What is the cause of the loss of international business?
   iii   What is a requirement for managers to do a good job?
   iv   Which groups of people outside their company do managers have to communicate with?

One criticism of UK managers is that relatively few speak a second language fluently. This can cause obvious problems for businesses that trade in a global market. Research suggests that UK companies lose around 13 per cent of the international deals they try to complete due to 'communication problems'. Managers also need effective written skills if they are to carry out their jobs effectively. The ability to quickly summarize key points in the form of a report for others in the business is of real value. So is the skill of reading a report written by someone else and being able to draw out the important elements. *factor, aspect*

As well as their own staff, managers have to work with other people too. They interact with customers, more senior managers, suppliers, trade union officials, government officials and the local community. Managers need to be comfortable in the company of diverse groups, and they need to able to communicate formally when required and to engage in informal small talk.

2   Complete summaries A and B with words from the corresponding passages below. Use NO MORE THAN ONE WORD for each answer.

> **Summary A**
> There should be a small number of (1) .... at meetings and there needs to be a (2) .... for any meeting, which will include a clear agenda. During the meeting there needs to be good (3) .... management and clarity about what the meeting should hopefully (4) .... At the end, there should be a summary and agreement about (5) .... action.

Passage A

Managers need a range of communication skills to carry out their jobs effectively. They need to be able to articulate their ideas and vision and to convey enthusiasm. Good managers may, at times, need to be able to argue points cogently and to persuade people to their point of view. However, good managers appreciate that communication is a two-way process, and that listening is an important element of communication. Listening to the views of others can help to test ideas as well as to develop new products and methods of production.

The most common forum in which managers are required to communicate are meetings. It is important for managers to plan for meetings, whether with a single person or with a group. Managers should not invite too many participants to keep numbers to a minimum. They should have a clear agenda for discussion and should exercise tight time controls to prevent meetings dragging on. Managers should enter each meeting with a clear idea of what they want it to achieve. At the end of a meeting it is good practice to summarize what has been agreed and what needs to happen in the future.

Summary B

Working with other people is not always easy, but it is (6) .... for the role of managers that they have interpersonal skills that are (7) .... Their (8) .... may need encouragement and help with (9) .... and solving problems between colleagues.

Passage B

Communication skills should not be taken for granted. Many managers require training in written and oral communication skills and many businesses would benefit from employing managers who speak at least one other language.

Interpersonal skills are also necessary if a manager is to work successfully with other people. If managers lack interpersonal skills, then they are likely to be of limited effectiveness in their role. Managers with effective interpersonal skills can motivate others and can co-ordinate the work of their employees. To do this, managers may need to coach and encourage employees as well as solving disputes and, perhaps more importantly, preventing conflict.

Progress check

How many boxes can you tick? You should work towards being able to tick them all.

Did you ...

remember to use your skim-reading and/or scanning skills to avoid having
   to read the whole passage?

notice the word limit and stick to it?

try to predict the type of word you were looking for?

Review 2

1   Answer the following questions about the previous units in NO MORE THAN FIVE WORDS. This will help you practise keeping to word limits.

   1   What was your favourite topic from units 4–6?

   2   What was the best exam tip you read in these units?

   3   What did you learn about nature from unit 5 that you did not already know?

   4   Have your feelings about the IELTS exam changed since starting to practise with this book? How?

2   Use these linking words to complete the text.

> also   in fact   for example   and   such as   although   however

(1) .... the communication process is always the same, it can take many different forms depending on the type of communication. (2) .... , in non-verbal communication, the code used could be gestures, body language, eye contact (3) .... facial expressions, (4) .... a smile.

From the above examples, it will be clear that communication is not just about the transfer of ideas; it is (5) .... about feelings and emotions.

In a business context, meetings are often conducted in quite a relaxed way, with participants using first names and informal language. (6) .... , as soon as the meeting is official, minutes will be kept, following a standard format. What may first seem an informal situation may, (7) .... , be more important than it looks.

Exam tip

You will understand a text better if you think about why the writer wrote it and who the text was written for.

3   Answer the following questions about the text in exercise 2 by choosing a, b, c or d.

   i   *Where do you think the passage first appeared?*

   a   in the introduction of an academic article

   b   in a beginners' textbook for business students

   c   in a general interest magazine aimed at young adults

   d   on a website from a business corporation

ii   *What was probably the main reason why the writer wrote the text?*

   a   to inform the reader about the topic of communication

   b   to inform the reader about the difficulties of relationships in business contexts

   c   to persuade the reader of his/her opinion about communication

   d   to question generally held beliefs about business communication

4   **Match the following words to make collocations that were mentioned in units 4–6.**

1	product	**a**	ad
2	facial	**b**	town
3	public	**c**	placement
4	advertising	**d**	pursuits
5	natural	**e**	process
6	newspaper	**f**	history
7	coastal	**g**	expression
8	communication	**h**	library
9	formal	**i**	information
10	women	**j**	agency
11	outdoor	**k**	explorers
12	veterinary	**l**	surgeon
12	financial	**m**	animal
14	marine	**n**	register

5   **Can you name the following objects or animals that you might see on a marine walk?**

1 .... 2 .... 3 .... 4 ....

6   **Correct the mistakes, if any, in the following sentences.**

   1   The secretary wrote the minutes of the meeting outlining the disagreements we reached.

   2   There are about seven billion people in the world. In fact, about 1.3 billion of them live in China.

   3   I always get ground under my fingernails when I am gardening.

   4   My aunt is the only sibling I have left.

   5   Pickling and drying are methods of food preservation.

7 Business management

Part 1: Vocabulary

1 Match the words to their definitions.

1 withdrawal *b*

2 pension *e*

3 pay slip *d*

4 overdraft *a*

5 mortgage

6 current account *h*

7 cheque *g*

8 fee *i*

9 fine *f*

a if you have this, you have spent more money than you have in your bank account, and so you owe the bank money

b an amount of money that you take from your bank account

c a sum of money that you pay to be allowed to do something

d a small piece of paper that shows how much an employer has paid you

e a regular sum of money received after retiring (= stopping work completely), given by an employer or by the state

f a punishment in which a person is ordered to pay a sum of money because they have done something illegal or broken a rule

g a printed form on which you write an amount of money and who it is to be paid to. Your bank then pays the money to that person from your account

h a personal bank account which you can take money out of at any time using your cheque book or cash card

i a loan of money which you get from a bank or building society in order to buy a house

2a Copy and complete the table on the next page by writing in the words that relate to the categories. Some relate to more than one category.

> ATM   withdrawal   cash point   salary   rent   purchase   pay slip   overdraft
> loan   investment   hole in the wall   fees   debit card   savings account   fines
> mortgage   credit card   cheque   automatic teller machine   owe

Saving money	Borrowing money from the bank	Getting your own money from the bank	Earning money	Paying money
savings account ATM *hole in the wall*	*credit card* loan *pay slip mortgage*	*debit card withdrawal cash point*	*salary rent*	*fines investment cheque*

2b Now underline four phrases in the 'getting your own money' category that have the same meaning.

2c Complete these sentences using words from exercise 2a.

1 I have to go to the *hole in the wall* before we go to the restaurant.

2 If you want to avoid paying a *fines*, you need to pay your taxes in time.

3 If your children attend private school, you need to pay school *fees*.

4 The bank has given me an ....: if I owe them less than £100 they won't charge me interest.

5 When I moved, I took out a .... over 25 years, but I hope to pay it back early.

Watch Out!

Although *few* and *a few* both mean 'not many', they are used quite differently:

few has a negative meaning. It emphasizes what is missing.

*There are **few** copies of this book.* = Not many copies exist, so you may not get one.

a few means, 'a small number'. It emphasizes what is (still) there.

*There are **a few** copies of this book.* = There aren't many copies but there are some, so you can still have one.

Note that *few* is normally used in a formal context.

3 Match the sentences 1–2 with their meaning a–b.

1 It should be noted that **there are a few theorists who believe that** this is the right way to do business.

a There are some theorists who believe that.

2 It should be noted that **there are few theorists who believe that** this is the right way to do business.

b It is difficult to find a theorist who believes that.

Exam information | Matching information

In the exam, you may be asked to match specific information, for example, a reason, a description or an explanation, to the section of a text where it can be found – A, B, C, etc.

Exam tip

Read the questions first, then skim-read the text to get an idea of its structure, and scan for the specific information. Every paragraph usually has a sentence that summarizes the main idea(s) in the paragraph (the topic sentence). This sentence may help you.

1 **Match the underlined parts in the text opposite to the type of specific information.**

> explanation   reason (x3)   example   comparison   condition

explanation: the companies that are quoted in the leading share price indices

2a **What are the following paragraphs about? Choose a, b or c.**

i *paragraph A*

    a the media   **b** large companies   **c** smaller businesses

ii *paragraph D*

    a the reasons why small companies are better than larger ones

    b the reasons why the government wants more small businesses

    c a list of good points about small companies

iii *paragraph E*

    a the role of policy makers

    b the importance of business planning

    c tips on improving your business

2b **Now decide which sentence in each of the paragraphs A, D and E is the topic sentence.**

3 **Underline the key words in these questions and then look for the answers in the text.**

    1 Which paragraph mentions statistics?

    2 In paragraph A, which word indicates that the text will not be about large businesses?

    3 In paragraph C, which sentence explains why new and developing small businesses are crucial to the success of the economy?

    4 Which paragraph builds on the same idea as the one in A and C (mentioned in question 5)?

(A) The business sections of the media tend to focus on large, traditional companies. By definition, these are high-profile businesses – the companies that are quoted in the leading share price indices. However, most economists agree that smaller businesses, particularly new and developing small businesses, are central to the long-term success of any economy. They argue that the industries of the future will originate in the small business sector. That is why the United Nations Economic Commission for Europe describes SMEs (small and medium-sized enterprises, with less than 250 employees) as 'the engine of economic development'.

(B) In the UK, the Department of Trade and Industry (DTI) reported that the total number of businesses, including small companies, partnerships and sole traders, rose by 260,000 in 2004 to 4.3 million (source: www.dti.gov.uk). This is up from the previous year and represents the best figures ever recorded.

(C) This is success for government policy. Successive UK governments have sought to encourage small business start-ups. Behind the policy is a belief that small businesses contribute to a stronger economic base, and that they have the ability to thrive in a competitive global business environment.

(D) The government also encourages small businesses because they are:
- a source of employment
- flexible and innovative
- responsive to gaps in the market
- able to accommodate people with a passion for a product who might not thrive in a large corporation.

Business planning

(E) Policy makers recognize that it is not sufficient to simply encourage an enterprise culture. If new entrepreneurs are to succeed, if new businesses are to thrive, then it is important that they appreciate the central role of planning. A business plan is the basis of new business development, and it encourages an entrepreneur to think ahead and plan, as far as possible, for the business to be successful.

(F) Writing a business plan will not in itself ensure that a business survives. However, it is an invaluable exercise, forcing entrepreneurs to go through planning steps to make sure their business propositions are viable. A business plan draws on concepts, skills and knowledge, including:
- doing market research to make sure that planned products and services meet customer needs
- understanding the market by analysing competitors' products, services and prices
- setting clear business aims and objectives
- finding sufficient capital to meet the business's short-term and long-term needs
- deciding on the most suitable structure and form of ownership for the business

Glossary

share price indices: plural of 'share price index': a system by which (the speed of) changes in the value of share prices is recorded and measured • *sole trader*: a person who owns their own business and does not have a partner or any shareholders.

Questions 1–6

The passage below has nine paragraphs A–I. Which paragraphs mention the following information? You may use any letter more than once.

1 physical and mental problems that a business owner can face ....

2 leadership and team improvement ideas ....

3 the advantage of not expanding in business ....

4 individuals and larger groups that are available to help people who are new to business ....

5 the reasons why the more basic jobs in a small company should not be not be carried out by employers ....

6 external reasons why companies should try to keep their employees' knowledge and expertise up-to-date ....

Setting up in business

(A) It takes a considerable commitment to set up and run a small business. Owners must be able to do all the tasks necessary to run the business or have sufficient funds to buy in appropriate external help, and even then they must be able to check the quality of the service they are receiving.

(B) Anyone planning to start a business must be realistic about what can be achieved, and in what time frame. Entrepreneurs often work extremely long hours, not just during 'trading' hours, but also after hours doing all the associated paperwork. If entrepreneurs overwork, they will find it difficult to make good decisions and will lack the energy to analyse and evaluate marketing and finance data. If an entrepreneur becomes over tired and over anxious, they can undermine their businesses by giving the impression that things are bad and the business is just about to close down.

(C) Many organizations provide support networks for entrepreneurs running small businesses. These networks provide training and access to experienced business mentors for little or no charge. The Business Link network, funded by Department of Trade and Industry, is one source of this kind of support. If entrepreneurs are under 30 years of age, the Prince's Trust also provides training and mentoring for business start-ups. There are various other privately run business networking groups which can be both fun and mutually supportive.

(D) Owners need to consider four key issues: training, leadership and team development, delegation and management systems.

(E) Investment in training is necessary to ensure that staff have the skills to do their jobs efficiently and they can meet the requirements of current legislation such as health and safety. Staff may also need training to develop skills to meet internationally recognized quality standards for products and service delivery. Research shows that small and medium-sized firms often find it very difficult to organize effective training.

(F) Ideally, workplace teams should be happy, creative working groups of individuals who support each other, work to each other's strengths and work towards the business's goals. This might require the owners to undertake self-assessment and target-setting reviews to ensure that the business is staying focused on its objectives. Team development can be fostered by organizing events such as team lunches and days out walking together.

(G) Owners should delegate and employ appropriate people to do the tasks that they cannot do or do not have time to do. By freeing themselves from some of the easier day-to-day tasks of the business, owners can spend their time monitoring the overall business and thinking about where the business should be going. Certainly if the owners are passionate about the business, they need time to step back and focus on the long-term goals and vision of the organization. They also need time to network, to build up sales leads and to explore further investment opportunities for the business.

(H) In time, owners need to be able to let go of control of some aspects of the business and to develop more formal management systems. This is probably the most difficult task for any entrepreneur. Many entrepreneurs find it very difficult to trust paid employees to run their businesses.

(I) At this stage in their development, without outside help and guidance, many businesses simply reach their 'natural' capacity and they do not develop or grow any further. Entrepreneurs need to decide whether they want to keep their business small – so that they retain control of all decisions – or whether they want to go on growing their business and therefore accept that this will necessarily change their role in the business.

Glossary

Business Link: the UK government's online resource to provide support for businesses • *Prince's Trust:* a charity in the UK started by Prince Charles in 1976 to help young people

Progress check

How many boxes can you tick? You should work towards being able to tick them all.

Did you …
remember to underline the key words in the questions? ☐
look for synonyms of the key words? ☐
look for topic sentences in the paragraphs? ☐
realize there was a glossary you could use? ☐

8 Young people's rights

AIMS: Vocabulary related to rights and responsibilities • Understanding sentence structure
• Matching sentence endings

Part 1: Vocabulary

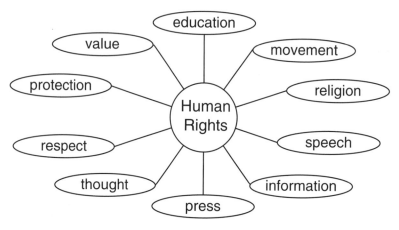

1a The following words are related to professional meetings and responsibilities. Write the words in the correct categories. Use a bilingual dictionary to help you.

> minutes (of a meeting)   election   committee   voting   secretary
> representative   nomination   member   council   chairperson

a group of people	a person	an object	an activity
member committee council	representative secretary chairperson	election nomination	voting election minutes

1b Complete the text with words from exercise 1a. There may be more than one possibility. You may need to change some words to plural.

Beech Lane School Parent ......*Committee*......

.... of the meeting held on October, 2012.

Apologies were received from Mrs Smart.
There were two points covered:

1   Because of the long-term absence of Mrs Smart, we will have a/an ...*an* ...*election*...
    for a new ...*chairperson*... to lead the meetings. We need all the ...*nomination*...

two weeks before the next meeting. Any .... who attends that meeting will be able to take part in the ....

2 The school fair was discussed. A list of duties was drawn up and will be sent to everybody by Friday. It's expected that everyone will do their best to help out on the day.

1c **Which words are being defined? Try to write the answers without looking back at the previous exercises.**

1 *Council* ....: a group of people that controls a group or organization

2 *Committee* ....: a group of people chosen or appointed to perform a specified service or function

3 *Secretary*: a person who handles correspondence, keeps records, and does general clerical work for an individual, organization, etc.

4 *members* ....: an official record of the proceedings of a meeting, conference, convention, etc.

5 *Chairperson*: a person who has authority at a meeting, a committee, a debate, a department, etc.

Watch out!

Immediately . Immediately.

In English, the normal word order is subject–verb–object, so we are used to seeing a verb and its subject together. However, sometimes the noun immediately before the verb is not the subject, so when you are skim-reading be careful to look at the whole subject.

The staff members who need to speak to the parents are not here today.
(It is not the parents, but the staff members, who need to speak to the parents, who are not here.)

The decision which was made by the school council is not popular.
(It is the decision made by the school council, not the school council, that is unpopular.)

2 **Read the sentences and answer the questions with the *full* subject. Then underline the most important noun in the subject.**

1 *The photographs of the people partying on the beach with my sisters are beautiful.*
Who or what are beautiful?

2 *The importance of the education I received in the UK should not be forgotten.*
What should not be forgotten?

3 *The details of the cases involving the teenagers who travelled without passports are not known yet.*
What is not known?

4 *The secret of a successful career, according to my mother, is to have children first, when you are still young.*
What is this sentence mainly about: the secret, a career or a mother?

Exam information | Matching sentence endings

In the exam, you may be given a number of incomplete sentences and you will need to complete them by choosing from a list of options. There will be more options than you need. The sentences will be in the same order as the information in the text.

Exam tip

Try to predict how each sentence will end before looking at the list of endings.

1a **Try to predict what type of word will come next in the following sentences. Choose from verb, noun, adjective, adverb or preposition. There may be more than one possibility.**

1 The African Charter on the rights and welfare of the …
2 It was chosen …
3 This Children's charter …
4 It covers the economic, social, political and cultural …
5 Education needs to be …
6 It needs to be delivered …

1b **Now use your predictions to match the sentence beginnings 1–6 with the correct endings a–f.**

1 The African Charter on the Rights and Welfare of the .c.   a by a national council.

2 The name was chosen a.   b in an efficient manner. *way*

3 This Children's charter f.   c child has existed for many decades.

4 It covers the economic, social, political and cultural e.   d thorough and consistent.

5 Education needs to be .d.   e rights of African children.

6 It needs to be delivered .b.   f was written in 1990.

Exam tip

The complete sentences need to be grammatically correct, but they also need to accurately reflect the information in the text. This is another type of exam task where focusing on the key words in the instructions and looking for synonyms and paraphrasing in the text will help. Look for the key words in the sentence beginnings, not the endings: you may not need to read through all the endings in detail, so don't waste your time!

2 The following text has been divided into four parts. For each part, choose the best sentence ending from a number of options.

i Human rights …

   a are about having everything you need and want.

   b apply especially to people with disabilities.

   c are about rights and also about freedoms. ✓

ii Human rights …

   a not before World War II.

   b are less important when there is a war.

   c are now an international issue. ✓

Human rights are ideas about what everyone is entitled to. Basic human rights include the right to life, and the right to food and clean drinking water. Others include the right to vote and to freedom of expression. In the UK, most people have their basic human rights met most of the time. However, in some countries people's freedoms may be limited. Also, in the UK, there are still areas of human rights that some people believe could be improved, such as the rights of people with disabilities.

The modern idea of human rights was developed after the Second World War, during which many people's rights were violated. On a large scale, these human rights abuses are known as war crimes. As a result, the United Nations (UN) was formed to provide a place for nations to resolve conflicts peacefully. It was set up by the Universal Declaration of Human Rights (UDHR), which consisted of 30 articles describing the basic rights of every person, and was signed in 1948 by 48 countries.

iii According to the Universal Declaration, it is an issue of fairness to be …

   a accepted everywhere in public.

   b educated. ✓

   c equal treatment.

The first section of the Universal Declaration states: 'All human beings are born free and equal in dignity and rights.'

Key rights relating to being 'born free' include freedom of speech and of movement, the right to a fair trial, and freedom from torture and from hunger.

Key rights relating to 'being equal' include a right to an education, and the right to be treated equally, without discrimination, in all areas of public life.

The Universal Declaration was designed as a safeguard to protect the human rights of people around the world.

iv The European Charter of Fundamental Rights …

   a resulted in social and technological changes.

   b included information about rights related to new technology.

   c replaced older declarations of human rights.

A legal basis for human rights

The European Convention of Human Rights was drawn up in 1963, giving a legal framework for human rights in the UK and other European countries. Here, people can complain to the European Court of Human Rights (or ECHR), based in Strasbourg, France. In 1998, the European Union (EU) decided to update the list of human rights, to take account of changes in society and technology. The result was the European Charter of Fundamental Rights (2000). This included some newer human rights:

- The right to a private life, including a right to privacy and to confidentiality of letters and emails.

- The right to limits on working hours and to have annual paid holiday.

- The right to respect the integrity of human beings, including a ban on financial gain from the human body. This includes the sale of human organs and the cloning of human beings.

- The right to data protection, which means that if a company holds data on you, you can ask where it got the information and what it is.

v If you are under 18 …

   a there should be economic, cultural and other rights.

   b you should obey the rules of the 1991 convention.

   c you have over 40 rights.

People aged 17 and under

For children and young people there is The United Nation's Convention on the Rights of the Child (UNCRC), which covers economic, social, cultural and political rights. The UK agreed to obey the rules of the convention in 1991, which means that every child in the UK, without exception, has certain rights that he or she is entitled to, more than 40 in total. Here are some examples:

- the right to life, survival and development

- the right to have their views respected, and to have their best interests considered at all times

- the right to a name and nationality, freedom of expression, and access to information concerning them

- the right to education, leisure, culture and the arts

Questions 1–5

Complete each sentence with the correct ending A–I.

1 Students' views are likely to be taken seriously if there are … ….……

2 Rules related to uniform are most likely to be discussed at … ….……

3 Year councils may get involved in … ….……

4 In the Year 8 council that is mentioned, teachers make sure that students are … ….……

5 Those in power are … ….……

A bullying and fundraising.

B more likely to bully others.

C not always the best listeners.

D not left on their own.

E organizing events.

F representative from the different year groups.

G school and year councils as well as peer mentoring schemes.

H school councils.

I teachers and parents of older students.

Participating in the school community

It is important that students' feelings, opinions and suggestions are listened to, taken into account, and that the right action is taken. There are a number of ways that this can be achieved, i.e. school councils, year councils and peer mentoring.

School councils

Most schools have a school council which exists to let the teachers and head teacher know what students' opinions are on a range of school issues. The school council usually consists of two or three elected representatives from each year group.

A school council might meet once or twice a month to discuss issues such as the dress code, the use of social areas, charity fundraising and bullying.

Year councils

Because school councils are sometimes dominated by older students, some schools have introduced year councils. The aim of a year council is to give students the opportunity to express opinions on matters of importance to that particular year group. The following is an example of the rules relating to a school's council for year 8 (pupils aged 12–13).

1 The council's purpose is to act as a forum for discussion of school issues relevant to Year 8, and to let the teachers and head teacher know what student opinion is on these issues. The council will also take responsibility for cooperating with year staff in the organization of one social event per term for Year 8.

2 Membership of the council will consist of three representatives from each class, elected on a termly basis.

3 Meetings will be held once a fortnight. The council members will elect a chair to control the meetings and a secretary who will be responsible for circulating the agenda for each meeting and taking and circulating minutes of meetings.

4 The class representatives will be responsible for giving a report of the council's meetings to their class. Agenda and minutes of meetings will be put up in each classroom.

5 The Year 8 council will elect two of its members to be members of the school council, with responsibility for raising issues on behalf of Year 8 students at school council meetings.

6 The chair, secretary and school council representatives will be responsible for taking up matters raised at council meetings with the year head and other teachers, and for reporting back on such matters to the Year 8 council.

7 The head of year will attend all council meetings as an observer and both they and the other year staff will be available as required to offer support and advice to council members and to assist in the settlement of disputes.

Peer mentoring

There are other ways in which students' voices can be heard. One of the most popular schemes involves peer mentoring. Those who express an interest receive training to become mentors so that they are better equipped to help others. This starts from primary school age, when the mentors may get involved in issues related to conflict resolution. At secondary school and at university, mentors are likely to deal with a larger variety of issues, such as educational and health-related matters.

The underlying belief in schemes like these is that being heard by your peers can be more effective and helpful as fellow students may have more time and understanding than teachers or others in authority.

Progress check

How many boxes can you tick? You should work towards being able to tick them all.

Did you …
read the sentence beginnings carefully? ☐
remember to underline the key words in the sentence beginnings? ☐
try to predict what could grammatically come next in the sentence? ☐
check carefully if the meaning of the sentence ending you chose
    corresponded exactly to what was said in the passage? ☐

9 Community matters

AIMS: Vocabulary about groups • Categorizing and labelling • Matching features

Part 1: Vocabulary

1 These pictures symbolize different aspects of 'community'. Complete these definitions of two-word phrases where the first word is 'community'. If necessary, choose it from the box below the table.

1 community …	a place that is specially provided for the people, groups and organizations in a particular area, where they can go in order to meet one another and do things
2 community …	an educational institution in the USA where students from the surrounding area can take courses in practical or academic subjects
3 community …	a system in which the police work only in one particular area of the community, so that everyone knows them. In Britain, there are Community Support Officers, volunteers who are trained to prevent and solve low level crimes so that people feel safer
4 community …	unpaid work that criminals sometimes do as a punishment instead of being sent to prison
5 community …	help available to persons living in their own homes, rather than services provided in residential institutions
6 community …	the feeling of loyalty to a group that is shared by the people who belong to the group

spirit   centre   college   service   policing   care

2 The word *community* contains information about its meaning and its grammatical category: it is similar to the word *common*, and the *-ity* ending tells us that the word is a noun.

What do you think the words in the table opposite mean? What are their grammatical categories? If you are not sure, choose from the options in the box below the table.

	grammatical category	meaning
communal		
a commune		
a communist		

(handwritten left margin: c, b, a next to the rows)

a	a supporter of communism (the political belief that all people are equal and that workers should control the means of producing things)
b	a group of people who live together and share everything.
c	belonging or relating to a community as a whole; something that is shared

3 Categorize the following words by ticking the appropriate column(s). There may be more than one correct answer. Then complete the other boxes in the table, where possible.

	adjective	verb	adverb	noun
criminal	✓		✓	✓
volunteer	✓	✓	✓	
loyalty	✓			✓
residential	✓	*Yesid*	✗	*resident*
punish	*Punishable*	*Punish*	*Puŷ*	*Punishment*

4 The words on the right refer to groups of people. Match them with the word on the left that they best combine with. Use a dictionary if necessary.

1	political *a*	**a**	party
2	online *f*	**b**	cast
3	voluntary *g*	**c**	band
4	film *b*	**d**	group
5	rock *c*	**e**	team
6	friendship *d*	**f**	community
7	sports *e*	**g**	organization

Watch Out!

It's important to recognize what pronouns in a text refer to. Be careful with *they, their* and *them*: they do not always relate to plural forms. They are often used to talk about individuals to avoid mentioning gender (*he, she, his* or *her, him* or *her*).

A team member must be prepared to put other people's needs before their own. (This avoids the use of 'his/her own'.)

Exam information | Matching features

In the exam, you may be asked to match a list of factual statements or opinions to a group of features taken from a text. The information in the list of statements will not be in the same order as in the text. You may not need all the features or you may be able to use some of them more than once.

1 Copy and complete the table, according to features they have in common, e.g. grammatical form or meaning. Then label each of the categories. (Hint: two of the columns are grammatical categories.)

organization he educational community communal team her cast practical crowd they loyal band academic she theirs criminal them safe mine party

Category 1:	Category 2:	Category 3:
organization	he	educational

2 Look at the newsletter on the next page. Choose one or two words from each paragraph (A–G) to describe what the paragraph is about. The first one has been done for you.

A *fundraising (walk)*   E ..... future damage
B trees   F ..... ~~tough~~
C ~~Volunteers~~ history   G ..... holiday
D ~~feasts~~ events

3 How many of the paragraphs mention the following? Write the letters A–G.

1 dogs ...... D
2 money ....
3 problems in the community ...... E
4 activities for children ...... F

5 activities that involve food ...... G
6 people who live(d) locally ...... A
7 volunteers ...... C B

4 Find paraphrases in the text for the following statements. Write them in your notebook.

1 As many people have been asking for it …
2 Many people turned up to the Forest Schools activities.
3 The winner will receive a big chocolate egg.
4 There will be another group meeting so that everyone can practise before the real interviews.
5 We have just planted many new trees.
6 You need to enrol before you can attend any of these activities.

Warley Woods Community Trust

Welcome to our third newsletter of the year!

(A) Our main activity for March is our *Walk for the Woods* fundraising event on Saturday, 17th March, starting any time between 10 a.m. and 2 p.m. In recognition of locally born Jack Judge, who wrote the song 'It's a long way to Tipperary' 100 years ago, we will be walking the distance between Warley Woods and Tipperary. It is indeed a long way—260 miles—so we need a lot of people to do a lot of 1 mile laps round the Woods. The more people that you can get to sponsor you, the more money we can raise to help look after our beautiful woodland. Sponsor forms are available from the shop at the Woods or on our website.

(B) Lots of new trees have gone in recently. The Sunday volunteers planted two beeches and an oak in the meadow last week. This was thanks to a grant from the Big Tree Plant and to Lisa and Gordon Whitaker whose friends gave money for the big trees instead of wedding presents. Thanks to everyone who took part including Lisa and Gordon and South Staffordshire plc who dug the big holes for us. (There is a DVD of one of the volunteers falling in—or was he pushed?)

(C) There were 15 volunteers at the Oral History Training Day which was led very ably by Julia Letts. Lots of issues were discussed and ideas considered. The group will be meeting again and will have the opportunity to do some practice interviews before starting to interview the local people who have offered to tell their stories. We are happy to hear from others who would like to be interviewed about their memories of the Woods for the project. If you or anyone you know is interested, please contact Viv Cole at the office. This project is funded by Heritage Lottery Fund.

(D) We already have sponsors for two of our events this year. Derek Spires, a local estate agent, is sponsoring *Theatre in the Woods* which this year is *Much Ado About Nothing* and will take place on Thursday, 14th June. Also, Companion Care Vets are sponsoring the Picnic. We are still looking for a sponsor for the *All about Dogs* event on 9th September, so if you, or any company you know, would like to do this, please get in touch with the office.

(E) The trustees have been giving some thought to ways of minimizing future damage to the fountain, and have decided to contact a specialist local firm to see what can be done about the graffiti.

(F) There was a huge response to the Forest Schools activities held at half term. These will be held again during the Easter holidays on the following dates: 4th, 5th and 11th April from 10 a.m. to 3 p.m. for over 8s. On 12th April from 10 a.m. to 12 noon there will be a Teddy Bears' Picnic for the under 8s. All sessions must be booked in advance and forms are available at the shop or office.

(G) Finally, don't forget the Easter Egg Roll on Bank Holiday Monday, 9th April, starting at 11 a.m. Bring your £1.00 entry money and your own hard-boiled and decorated egg to roll down the hill in the woods. The first past the finishing line will win a massive chocolate egg! This year, due to popular demand, there will also be an Adults' Easter Egg Roll following the children's competition.

We look forward to seeing you all soon, at one of our many events!

Glossary

trust: a group of people or an organization that has control of an amount of money or property and invests it on behalf of other people or as a charity • *trustee:* someone with legal control of money or property that is kept or invested for another person, company or organization.

Questions 1–9

Match each item 1–9 with the correct group A–D. You can use any letter more than once.

1   people feel safe here   ....
2   these exist in different forms   ..~~B~~........
3   people support each other   ..~~B~~.....
4   it is difficult to say exactly what they are   ....
5   they have a lot to offer their members   ....
6   people can do things on a bigger scale   ....
7   the members meet up in person   ..~~B~~.....
8   people are prepared to take on other people's responsibilities   ....
9   people are strangers   ..~~D~~.....

> This is true for:
> **A**   all communities
> **B**   online communities
> **C**   traditional communities
> **D**   none of the mentioned communities

The importance of community

A   'Community' is not a concept that is easy to define. In this essay, I will examine what transforms individuals into a community, and discuss some different types. I will also look at what all communities have in common, the benefits they offer and draw conclusions about their increasing importance.

C   The word 'community' may trigger images of traditional communities in the developing world, where large families live together. Elderly parents live with their children and grandchildren in one house. Parents have relative freedom: if they leave the house there is always someone left behind to look after their children. If it is their own parents who need to support, their older children can take care of this. We may also imagine the neighbours as people who are happy to help out whenever it is needed. The stereotypical view is that of a village, where people have little but can feel very rich because everyone takes responsibility for the welfare of the others.

B   At the other end of the spectrum, there are other types of communities: ultra-modern ones, where the community members are unlikely to have actually met each other. These are online communities, where people blog or chat about particular issues that are important to them. They come across others on websites and may develop a relationship there with like-minded people, discussing the same topics. The view is often that these are artificial bonds between people who are, in effect, still isolated strangers.

B In reality, of course, this is not true, as the connections are real. Moreover, there are many types of communities in between these extremes: people who join sports and leisure clubs, who sign up with voluntary, political, religious or other organizations, who attend events such as coffee mornings (e.g. fundraising circles, mother and baby groups), or who take part in group discussions in their local area. They may be campaigning about issues or simply getting together for companionship and support.

B Human beings are social by nature, so it should not be a surprise that we organize ourselves in groups. However, there is more going on: these groups provide something that we cannot achieve on our own. The main benefit of being part of a larger group is strength in numbers. For example, we can access and share more information, we can take part in team sports, we can complain and campaign more effectively and even if we are just having a chat, online or in person, we can feel supported in whatever we do.

D The stereotypical views of the happy village and the isolated computer users may not be completely true, but what we do know is that whatever forms communities take, what defines them is the sense of identity and security that they provide for their members: the knowledge that there are people who we have something in common with and who can be relied on to be there when we need each other.

Progress check

How many boxes can you tick? You should work towards being able to tick them all.

Did you …
identify the key words in the statements?
look for paraphrases in the text?
scan the text to find the right section?

Review 3

1 Answer the following questions about units 7–9. *unit 9*
Community matters

1 What was your favourite topic from units 7–9?
2 What was the best exam tip you read in these units? *match*
3 What financial vocabulary can you remember from unit 7?
4 Can you explain the difference between *few* and *a few*?
5 How many nouns can you remember that can go after the word *community*?

2 Find (near) synonyms of the following words in the essay below. Try to do this within three minutes. This will help you practise working under timed conditions.

courageous	decline	disappearing	encourage	first
global	importance	increasing	level	vital

> *The country needs small and medium-sized companies now more than ever. Discuss.*
>
> When we read the newspapers, it seems like the world is made up of large multi-national companies, such as Starbucks, Apple and Google. Although these certainly contribute to the economy on a large scale, we should not underestimate the long-term value of small and medium-sized enterprises. After all, these might become the international brands of the future, while helping to maintain the economy in the meantime.
>
> It is this argument which is the reason for the many schemes and the different forms of help that the government has traditionally provided for start-ups, completely new businesses operating at a local level. They provide, for example, financial incentives, low business rents and help with writing a business plan. Other examples are the provision of business consultants who help with the initial market research, the analysis of competitors' products and prices, and advise on company structure. At a time where government money is drying up, it is important that this support continues.
>
> It is especially in a recession that we need brave people with big ideas, who are willing to take a risk to fill a gap in the market or to respond to a growing consumer need. These entrepreneurs are people who provide employment to their local community. In other words, they promote economic growth by investing in others as well as themselves.
>
> If local and national governments are prepared to invest in new businesses, they are also investing in the economic growth of the country. The better the support, the more likely it will be that the business will become one of the 40% of companies that survive their first five years in business. Surely that is exactly what is needed in these times of economic downturn.

3 Match the beginning and ending of the following sentences. If there is more than one grammatical possibility, think about the meaning.

1 Starbucks and Google are ...   **a** to the economy.

2 We need ...   **b** for employers.

3 Entrepreneurs are vital ...   **c** investment in local businesses.

4 Support is always important ...   **d** to survive their first year in business.

5 Every business wants ...   **e** global brands.

4 Finish the following sentences. You can use your own ideas, as long as the sentence is grammatical. Compare your answers to the complete sentences, which can be found in the text on the opposite page.

1 We should not underestimate ...

2 It is this argument which ...

3 It is important that ...

4 We need people who are willing ...

5 These are people who provide employment to ...

6 They promote economic growth by ...

7 They are also investing ...

8 The better the support, the ...

5 Correct the mistakes, if any, in the following sentences.

1 In my community, there are few problems with graffiti, but not very many.

2 If one of my students has disorganized notes, I know they will have problems revising.

3 I dislike it when I have to use a communal bathroom.

4 The customer service assistant who wanted to speak to this customer is not here today, so I have asked the customer to speak to somebody else.

5 The person who is standing next to my sister is taller than her, but only because they are wearing a hat.

6 Label the following pictures. The words were all mentioned in unit 9.

1 rock band   2 online community   3 sport team   4 Policing

10 British culture

Part 1: Vocabulary

1a **Quiz: Match these names of buildings in London with their descriptions.**

1 City Hall

a This building is also known as London's Central Criminal Court or Justice Hall, and was named after the road it was on.

2 The Old Bailey

b This is the building where the two houses of Parliament of the United Kingdom, the House of Lords and the House of Commons, are based.

3 The Gherkin

c This building is home to the Mayor of London, and the regional administrative authority, consisting of over 600 members of staff. It is located near the River Thames, where it contrasts strongly with more traditional looking buildings.

4 The Palace of Westminster

d This is an office building, based at 30 St Mary Axe. It got its name because it is shaped like a vegetable.

1b **Label the pictures with the names of the buildings in exercise 1a.**

1 .... 2 .... 3 .... 4 ....

2 **Complete the text below. You can look at the words in the box below, but only if you need to.**

In England, 'Put the (1) .... on' is a phrase heard often, as people enjoy stopping for a (2) .... of tea and perhaps a biscuit. This daily ritual becomes much more formal in a (3) .... or hotel setting. If you go out for cream tea, you may get loose tea, brewed in a (4) .... and served at your table. This is accompanied by scones with cream and (5) .... There are different regional (6) .... about how cream tea is served. In Devon, they tend to put the cream on the scone first, with strawberry jam on top, whereas in Cornwall they spread (7) .... on the scone first and put the jam on before the cream. A traditional afternoon tea would also be accompanied with delicate (8) .... , such as cucumber, egg, ham and smoked (9) .... , as well as cakes. However you choose to accompany it, remember that in England, ordinary tea is always drunk with (10) ....

> butter   cup   customs   tearoom   jam   kettle   milk   salmon   sandwiches   teapot

3a Copy and complete the table by writing the following words in the right categories. Use a dictionary or check the meanings in the Answer key.

> Cornish pasty   bitter   duck-duck-goose   scones   haggis
> hopscotch   scotch   rarebit   leek   British bulldog

food	drink	activity
leek *rarebit* *scones* *haggis*	*scotch* *bitter*	*duck-duck-goose* *hopscotch* *british bulldog*

(handwritten: Cornish Pasty)

3b Two of the items in exercise 3a are typically associated with Scotland, two with Wales, and two with England. Which ones are they?

Scotland	Wales	England
		Cornish pasty

Watch out!

Do you know the difference between the United Kingdom, England, Great Britain and the British Isles? Which ones include Scotland and Wales? If you don't know, you may misunderstand exactly what an author is writing about. You could also cause offence to people in certain areas by using the wrong word! Check the Answer key to the next exercise if you are confused.

4 Identify the following on the map:

- England
- Scotland
- Wales
- Northern Ireland
- Ireland
- Republic of Ireland
- Great Britain
- the UK

Exam information | Matching headings

In the exam, you may be given a list of headings, and a text divided into sections. The headings will be in the form of short statements which summarize the information in a section. You will need to read the text sections and decide which of the headings best fits that section. This type of task tests whether you understand the organization of texts and can identify the main idea or topic in a paragraph.

1a To focus on this type of task, underline the main point in box A (the introduction). Then check your answer in the key before continuing.

1b Read all the paragraphs that follow and underline any evidence that links to this main point. Notice how one main theme is developed throughout the text.

1c Explain how the meaning of each of the following phrases is related to the overall theme of the text. The first one is done for you.

moreover (in A): introduces another reason why it is difficult to compare styles/periods

first of all (in B)   secondly (in B)   last but not least (in B)

despite (in C)   then again (in C)   moreover (in C)

unsurprisingly (in D)

1d We can say that each of the paragraphs B–D exemplifies the general theme with an example of a particular period. What is the example in each of these paragraphs?

1e The text has no conclusion. Look at the following suggestions for the conclusion of this text and cross out any that are not suitable.

The conclusion could:

  a pick up the point about how easy it is to be confused (i.e. the fact that different words refer to the same period and that the same words can refer to different periods)

  b refer back to the three main examples in paragraphs A–D

  c mention that non-British people may find it harder to understand the vocabulary relating to artistic styles

  d give information about another period (e.g. introduce the Elizabethan period)

  e include a personal opinion or comment relating to the main idea, or its consequences (e.g. visitors to the UK may need more information about tourist attractions than we might think)

A

It is not easy to compare the artistic styles and periods of different countries, especially as they may use different words to refer to the same features, and perhaps occasionally also use the same words with a slightly different meaning. Moreover, particular styles and periods overlap.

B

An example of this is the 'Victorian' period in Britain, which has a style that is often described as romantic. First of all, the name of this period links it immediately with British royal history, which potentially creates confusion to non-British people who may not be aware that the reign of Queen Victoria relates to approximately the second half of the 19th century. Secondly, despite the fact that Queen Victoria died in 1901 the style itself continued into the 20th century. And last but not least, it can be argued that there are distinctly different styles which can all be referred to as Victorian, e.g. the use of flower motifs and pastel colours.

C

Despite Victorian times being characterized by romanticism, the famous British romantic poets belong to the period before Queen Victoria. These are poets such as Robert Burns, William Wordsworth, Samuel Taylor Coleridge and John Keats. From the same era date famous writers such as Jane Austen and Mary Shelley (who wrote Frankenstein), and great architects such as James Wyatt and John Nash. The great painters Gainsborough, Reynolds, Turner and Constable can also be categorized in this period. But who outside of Britain could label this era? And, even if we know they can all be described as Georgian artists, which King George does this refer to? Actually, it refers to four of them (George I, George II, George III and George IV), and thus spans a long period incorporating most of the 18th century and some of the 19th. But then again, there was a Georgian revival in the 20th century, which means the label can also relate to that. Moreover, the style itself incorporates previous styles, including gothic, and has its own subdivision, Regency style, which describes the period of George IV.

D

The period after the Victorian era is referred to as Edwardian, after Edward VII who reigned from 1901 to 1910, when he died. Nobody is sure whether 1910 is the correct end point for the period, with some people suggesting it should be 1912, when the Titanic sank, the start of World War I (1914), its end (1918), or the signing of the post-war peace treaty of Versailles (1919). Elsewhere in Europe, the Art Nouveau era ended around the same time, and unsurprisingly, Art Nouveau is also used to describe the style which was common in Britain at that time. Floral motifs were very common … now where have I heard about that before?

2 Read the following paragraphs about British castles. Choose the best heading from the options.

Beaumaris castle is an impressive castle, built by King Edward I. It is considered one of the most beautiful medieval castles in Wales, probably because of its symmetrical shapes, but its purpose was military, the pretty geometrical shapes being rings of defense. Work started as early as 1295, but although it was done at a fast speed, it was never completed because of lack of money.

Scotland is right to be proud of Edinburgh castle. It dominates the city of Edinburgh from high up on its rock. The history of Castle Rock goes back all the way to the late Bronze Age (900 BC), when there were already people living there. In the middle ages it became a royal castle, and this lasted until the 17th century. In the 18th century it became an army base, but it is now mainly known as a visitor attraction.

a Beaumaris: a castle of contrasts
b Beaumaris: a typical medieval castle
c Beaumaris: the oldest Welsh castle

a Is Edinburgh the oldest castle in Britain?
b Edinburgh Castle: Scotland's pride and joy
c Edinburgh Castle and its many roles

1 The reading passage has five sections, A–F. Choose the correct heading for sections A–F from the list of numbered headings below. Write the correct number i–x next to sections A–F.

List of headings

i the disappearance of traditional playground sports

ii the disappearance of classic playground games

iii the dangers of the playground

iv the best traditional games in Britain

v possible explanations for the bans

vi not a very British bulldog

vii no real support for the bans

viii differing opinions about the bans

ix different ways of playing

x a closer look at some traditional games

Sections

Section A: ....

Section B: ....

Section C: ....

Section D: ....

Section E: ....

Section F: ....

Is this the end of traditional British playground pastimes?

Section A

A survey has suggested that traditional pastimes are increasingly being banned at break times in primary schools. Number one on the list is chasing game British Bulldog, followed by leapfrog and conkers.

Section B

Despite its name, British Bulldog is a game that does not involve animals, and is played all over the world in a number of variations. In its basic form it involves runners trying to get to the other side of the playground without being caught by the chaser, the 'bulldog'. If caught, they become a bulldog too, until there is only one person left: the winner of the game. 'Conkers' on the other hand, is genuinely British, as it is a game that was invented in England. The players bring their own 'conker': a horse chestnut attached to a thick piece of string that goes through the middle of the nut and is knotted underneath. Players pair up, wrap the string around one of their hands and try up to three times to hit the other person's conker by swinging their hand back and forth. They take this in turns until one of the conkers is destroyed. That could be the end of the game, or the winner could go on to 'fight' others. There are different types of scoring methods in place. The game is also played outside the school playground, with a world championship taking place in England every year.

Section C

It will come as no surprise that people have had accidents resulting in a broken arm or leg while playing British Bulldog, or by simply walking across the playground when a game is taking place! It is also not difficult to imagine that many conker players manage to hit their opponent's hand rather than their conker. Horse chestnuts are very hard and being hit with one hurts, as many school children will – proudly – tell you.

Section D

This whole situation is not new. In the past, we have also heard stories about the banning of kiss chase and of musical chairs. There is also anecdotal evidence that some schools ban marbles, and even hopscotch, duck-duck-goose and skipping. The main reason for forbidding these games is again fear of injury. Sometimes the justifications are stranger and perhaps not actually true. For example, kiss chase, a chase game where the person who has been caught receives a kiss before becoming the chaser, may pass on germs. And conkers might also be a problem for children with nut allergies.

Section E

Sporting activities are also becoming rarer on the playground, often because there is a lack of staff available to supervise them. Apart from banning these, there are also more original solutions, such as allowing students to play touch rugby only – a form of rugby where tackles are not allowed, and playing football with a soft ball rather than the traditional leather one. Having said that, these activities are often not popular with the kids, and this may discourage them from playing at all.

Section F

Your comments:

This is just ridiculous! Illnesses and injuries are part of growing up! *Sean, Watford*

I used to play all these games, and more. I think I split my lip once when I fell over during a circle game, but so what? It can't compete with the hours of fun I had with my friends. *Susan, Bournemouth*

I don't think it's wrong to question whether we should allow violent games in schools. After all, violence should not be tolerated in an educational environment. Perhaps this is something that could lead to healthy group discussions involving teachers and pupils about rules and behaviour, but in my opinion this should not result in a ban of healthy running games such as circle, tag or chase games. Otherwise all P.E. and sports activities should also be banned on health and safety grounds, which would be mad: it's just not necessary to do any of this. *Kiran, Cardiff*

Let's ban active playground activities. Let's keep the kids inside the classrooms during break times and pay extra staff to stay indoors to supervise them and keep them safe. Let's watch them become very fat and very boring adults! *A. Watson, Sheffield*

Allowing children to play games that involve the occasional risk, such as British Bulldog, teaches them to make intelligent decisions about their safety. *Mohammed, Scotland*

I blame lawyers and society: we always feel somebody should be to blame if anything goes wrong, so we can sue them for a lot of money. *Alison, London*

Glossary

leapfrog: a game that children play, in which a child bends over, while others jump over their back. • *a horse chestnut:* the nut of a horse chestnut tree (a large tree which has leaves with several pointed parts and shiny reddish-brown nuts) • *marbles:* a children's game played with small balls, usually made of coloured glass, in which you roll a ball along the ground and try to hit an opponent's ball

Progress check

How many boxes can you tick? You should work towards being able to tick them all.

Did you …
skim-read the sections first, one by one? ☐
underline key words? ☐
consider the main point of each paragraph? ☐
consider the overall text organization? ☐

11 Crime detection

AIMS: Vocabulary related to crime • Identifying information • Adjusting reading speed • True/False/ Not Given questions

Part 1: Vocabulary

1　　　　　2　　　　　3　　　　　4

1 The pictures show common objects which are used as weapons in a famous murder mystery game. Match the pictures to the words.

...*4*.... spanner ....lead pipe ....rope ...*1*.....candlestick

2a The following are idioms related to crime. Match them with their meanings.

d **1** to keep your nose clean   **a** when you are charged a great deal of money for something and you think this is unfair or unreasonable (British, informal)

h **2** to get a slap on the wrist   **b** to run away to avoid paying for something or to escape trouble (slang)

g **3** to face the music   **c** to do whatever you like without anyone controlling or punishing you (informal)

f **4** to be above board   **d** to behave well and stay out of trouble (informal)

b **5** to do a runner   **e** something that was bought at little cost (informal)

e **6** it was a steal   **f** to be in the open, without dishonesty

c **7** to get away with murder   **g** to put yourself in a position where you will be punished or criticized

a **8** it's daylight robbery   **h** to get a light punishment

2b Choose the correct sentence ending a, b or c.

　i *It's daylight robbery: they want to charge me*

　　a £15 for a teddy bear.

　　b £15 for a gold necklace.

　　c £15 for a holiday in Turkey.

ii   *I can't believe I had dinner in a nice restaurant but my date did a runner and …*
   a   I had to pay the bill for both of us.
   ⓒ   is very sporty.
   b   arrived late.

iii   *She went to court and got a slap on the wrist:*
   a   20 years in prison.
   ⓒ   12 hours of community service.
   b   three years in prison.

iv   *It was a steal: I paid*
   a   £15 for a teddy bear.
   c   £15,000 for a diamond ring.
   ⓑ   £150 for a holiday in Turkey.

v   *She has kept her nose clean for three years now and*
   a   is feeling much better.
   b   has not been caught by the police in that time.
   ⓒ   has not done anything illegal in that time.

vi   *When he gets home, he'll have to face the music because*
   a   I want to have a word about the money he has spent.
   b   I want to let him listen to the album I bought.
   c   I want to tell him about my mistakes.

vii   *She's been getting away with murder but*
   a   she has not gone to court yet.
   b   she'll have to do all her own washing from now on.
   c   she is not normally a violent person.

2c   **Complete these sentences with idioms from exercise 2a. You may have to make some changes to the form.**

1   It's difficult in this area to .... but neither of my children have ever had to speak to the police.
2   You want me to pay £8.50 for postage costs? That's .... 8 ....!
3   She lived there for eight weeks without paying rent and basically ....
4   I know I'll have to .... later but it's worth it to stay out until 4 a.m.
5   I can't believe he stole my dog and all he got from the judge was ...... 2 ....
6   She says it's .... 4 .... , even though most people think she is not allowed to charge an entrance fee.
7   I once waited more than half an hour for the bill to arrive in a restaurant and I nearly .... 5 ....
8   Come on, ladies, I'm selling watches for under £10 - surely that's ..it was   a steal .
                                                                              6

Exam tip

Don't waste too much time on unknown words: sometimes you don't need them. When it is useful, have a guess. But be careful too: remember that idioms are not to be taken literally.

3   **Which of the following is NOT a synonym of 'in prison'?**

in gaol	in the slammer	locked up	behind bars	serving time
in jail	doing time	closing time	imprisoned	

Exam information | True/False/Not Given

In the exam, you may be asked whether information is correct or not. You will be given a list of statements. If the text confirms the statement, your answer should be 'TRUE'. If the text contradicts the statement your answer should be 'FALSE'. If it is impossible to know from the text if the statement is true or not, your answer should be 'NOT GIVEN'.

Do not use your own opinion to answer but check in the text.

1 Do the sentences on the left provide answers to the questions on the right? Put a tick when they do, or write NOT GIVEN if they don't. Use only the information in the statements.

Sentences		Questions	✓ or NOT GIVEN
Fingerprints have been found that date back thousands of years to the time of the ancient Egyptians.	1	Do we have computers that help us determine how old fingerprints are?	N
	2	Did the ancient Egyptians live thousands of years ago?	✓
In 1910, Edmond Locard set up what is thought to be the first police crime laboratory in Lyons in France.	3	Is Edmond Locard French?	N
	4	Is Lyons in France?	✓
DNA fingerprinting was first used in the1980s when it was used as evidence to convict murderer Colin Pitchfork.	5	Was DNA fingerprinting technically possible in 1990?	✓
	6	Did Colin Pitchfork commit murder?	N

2 Read the statements below and write TRUE if the text next to it confirms the information, FALSE if it contradicts the information, or NOT GIVEN if there is not enough information.

Text		Statements	TRUE/FALSE/ NOT GIVEN
The Scenes of Crime Officers (SOCOs) that seal off (= stop people from entering), record and collect evidence from crime scenes are people employed by police forces but not police officers themselves.	1	SOCO means Scenes of Crimes Officer.	✓
	2	Recording and collecting evidence is important police work.	X
	3	SOCOs analyze evidence from crime scenes.	N
SOCOs are called to crime scenes at any time of the day or night, and may have to remain there for days or even weeks so that every piece of evidence is collected.	4	SOCOs have a difficult job to do.	.
	5	SOCOs work regular hours.	X
	6	After a crime, the SOCO's work continues until the crime is solved.	
Many SOCOs now use photographic and surveying techniques to produce virtual reconstructions of crime scenes that help with their recording and investigation of the scene.	7	SOCOs need to be able to take photographs.	✓
	8	After a crime, the crime is sometimes 'reconstructed' by actors.	⊥
	9	SOCOs have to record and investigate crime scenes.	✓

3 Make a note of your starting time. Read Part 1 as fast as you can, but make sure you understand what you read. Don't stop for unknown vocabulary. Afterwards, check your understanding by answering the questions. Make a note of the time when you finish.

Then do the same for Part 2. Check if you managed to complete Part 2 faster than Part 1.

Part 1
Crime-fighting technology: a necessity?

Crime-fighting technology is getting more sophisticated and rightly so. The police need to be equipped for the 21st century. In Britain we've already got the world's biggest DNA database. By next year, the state will have access to the genetic data of 4.25m people: one British-based person in 14. Hundreds of thousands of those on the database will never have been charged with a crime.

True or False? Most people in Britain are on the British DNA database.

Britain is also reported to have more than four million CCTV (closed circuit television) cameras. There is a continuing debate about the effectiveness of CCTV. Some evidence suggests that it is helpful in reducing shoplifting and car crime. It has also been used to successfully identify terrorists and murderers. However, many claim that better lighting is just as effective to prevent crime, and that cameras could displace crime. An internal police report said that only one crime was solved for every 1,000 cameras in London in 2007. In short, there is conflicting evidence about the effectiveness of cameras, so it is likely that the debate will continue.

True or False? CCTV has helped solve some small and large crimes.

Professor Mike Press, who has spent the past decade studying how design can contribute to crime reduction, said that, in order for CCTV to have any effect, it must be used in a targeted way.

True, False or Not Given?
Mike Press has been studying the link between design and the amount of crime for ten years.

Part 2
Most schemes that simply record city centres continually – often not being watched – do not produce results. CCTV can also have the opposite effect of that intended, by giving citizens a false sense of security and encouraging them to be careless with property and personal safety.

True or False? CCTV can make people feel safe, which can put them in more danger.

Professor Press said: 'All the evidence suggests that CCTV alone makes no positive impact on crime reduction and prevention at all. The weight of evidence would suggest the investment is more or less a waste of money unless you have lots of other things in place.' He believes that much of the increase is driven by the marketing efforts of security companies who promote the crime-reducing benefits of their products. He described it as a 'lazy approach to crime prevention' and said that authorities should instead be focusing on how to alter the environment to reduce crime.

True or False? Professor Press believes that CCTV can help reduce crime but only if there are also changes to the environment.

But in reality, this is not what is happening. Instead, police are considering using more technology in the future. Police forces have recently begun experimenting with cameras in their helmets. The footage will be stored on police computers, along with the footage from thousands of CCTV cameras and millions of pictures from number plate recognition cameras used increasingly to check up on motorists.

True, False or Not Given? The police are already using more technology than before.

Crime detection

Exam tip

You should adjust your reading speed throughout the exam. When you are looking for detailed information (e.g. the writer's opinion), you will need to slow down to make sure you find the exact answer. When you are asked for more general information (e.g. matching paragraph headings), you may be able to read faster. By practising, you will find the ideal balance between reading slowly enough to understand and fast enough to finish on time.

Questions 1–8

Do the following statements agree with the information in the text? Write:

TRUE	if the text confirms the statement
FALSE	if the text contradicts the statement
NOT GIVEN	if it is impossible to know from the text

Statements:

1 The police may ask the people who are at the crime scene to wait together until they can talk to them. ......F...........

2 SOCOs are not normally first at a crime scene. ....T.......

3 Sometimes hair, skin cells, etc. from a SOCO are left at the crime scene, even though they wear protection to try to stop this. ....not..........

4 Every item at a crime scene is photographed five times. ....F..........

5 Fibres are an example of trace evidence. ......T..........

6 If evidence is burnt, it cannot be dealt with. ....not....

7 A SOCOs job is to help get good evidence to court. ......T..........

8 SOCOs may have to go to court to provide evidence. ....not..

Investigating a crime scene

Assessing the scene

On arrival, the police officer's first job is to carry out an initial assessment of the scene. If they are at first unsure whether or not a crime has taken place, it's best to assume that it has. Valuable time and evidence in the investigation could be lost otherwise. First they must deal with anyone at the scene needing medical help. Any other people present at the scene must be kept apart, as they may be eyewitnesses or suspects. Witnesses at crime scenes are not allowed to talk to each other. A person's perception of what happened can get distorted during conversation.

The police officer then calls for a Scene of Crime Officer (SOCO).

Preserving the scene

When the SOCO arrives at the crime scene, they put on a full protective body suit, gloves, a mask, and plastic overshoes. Without this, the SOCO's skin cells, hair, fibres, fingerprints or shoeprints could be added to the crime scene.

Recording the scene

The SOCO must produce a permanent record of the crime scene, using detailed written notes, sketches, photographs and videos. It is essential that the original position of items at the scene is recorded. Some biological and chemical evidence may quickly deteriorate. Other evidence may be very fragile, and might be destroyed as the SOCO tries to recover it. Other evidence from the scene of crime will be sent to the forensic lab for analysis.

Photographing the scene

When photographing a crime scene, the SOCO follows four rules:

1 Photograph the whole crime scene.

2 Photograph each item at the scene before doing anything to it.

3 Add a scale and photograph the item again.

4 After collecting trace evidence from the item, or removing it for analysis, photograph the same part of the crime scene again.

The search for evidence

Any evidence at the crime scene may turn out to be important at some stage in the investigation, so it's important that the team's search is thorough and systematic.

- Some of the evidence, such as a cigarette butt, may be immediately obvious to the SOCO.

- Some of the evidence, such as fibres, may be present in very small amounts. This is called trace evidence.

- Other evidence, such as fingerprints, may be invisible to the naked eye, and special techniques are needed to reveal it.

- Some evidence may have been damaged, for example burnt. Special procedures are then needed.

Storing the evidence P2

Each item of evidence must be packaged separately, labelled and sealed before it is stored. Small items, such as hairs, fibres, glass fragments and paint, are put into plastic bags or bottles and sealed. Clothing and shoes are put into paper sacks. Evidence must be stored in secure facilities. Most types of evidence are kept in cool, dry rooms. Biological samples are refrigerated or frozen to prevent their decay.

Using the evidence in a criminal investigation

SOCOs must always use standard methods to process evidence. Only then will it provide valid information that can be used, or be admissible, in court. If fingerprint and DNA evidence are absent, incomplete or damaged, other types of evidence may be very important in solving the crime. The way in which the SOCO team searches for, collects, packages and stores such evidence is important in preserving it. Badly preserved evidence may not provide useful information for the investigation and may not be admissible in court.

Progress check

How many boxes can you tick? You should work towards being able to tick them all.

Did you …

think about your reading speed and adjust it if necessary?

focus on detail? A general topic can be mentioned but the answer can still be *Not Given* if the exact information is not in the text.

12 Travel

Part 1: Vocabulary

1   Label the pictures.   motorway   country lane   dual carriageway   path

1 .... 2 .... 3 .... 4 ....

2   Circle the best word.

1 A *runway / motorway / street* is a major road that has been specially built for fast travel over long distances, which has several lanes and special slip roads to enter and exit.

2 A *bridge / pavement / path* is a way between two places that people can walk along.

3 A *main road / dual carriageway / freeway* is the British equivalent for what the Americans call a 'divided highway': a road which has two lanes of traffic travelling in each direction with a strip of grass or concrete down the middle to separate the two lots of traffic.

4 A *country lane / cycle lane / pavement* is a narrow road, usually in a beautiful location.

3a   Read this blog about the daily commute (a journey made regularly between one's home and one's place of work). Underline all the phrases that relate to places and highlight the ones that refer to travel or transport. Do not use a dictionary.

commuter101 Is anybody else fed up with roadworks? Is it just here in London where they are appearing all at once, or is it the same everywhere? It's added an hour to my journey. EACH WAY.

Heather98 Pretty much the same here, commuter 101. I have to do a round trip of 20 miles between Cheltenham and Birmingham every day and pass (very slowly!) 3 areas with roadworks, on different parts of the M5. It's doubling the time it takes me to get to and from work.

Musicfan2 Take a train, guys. Last time I checked trains were going regularly between Cheltenham and Birmingham. And in London you've got the tube.

CharlotteL. t's driving me crazy too. There are roadworks near the service station by Junction 9 on the M6. It's like the traffic is at a standstill there. I try to avoid it but it's not always possible.

Heather98 @ Musicfan2: not an option, I'm afraid. I am a sales rep and need my car during the day.

chico I agree with Musicfan. Instead of complaining about roadworks, the cost of petrol, the price of cars etc. we need to think about other options. And I don't mean car sharing or building more motorways. I say we try to save our environment by campaigning for better bus and train networks and for different types of public transport such as trams. Use your time and anger to try and make a difference!

commuter101 What time? I'm stuck in a traffic jam!! (☺)

3b **Look back at the blog in exercise 3a and find the following:**

1 A phrase, used in informal language, that means 'to be tired of something'
2 An informal phrase that means 'almost'
3 A phrase that means 'a trip to a place and back again'
4 Names of two motorways in Britain
5 A phrase that refers to places in Britain that sell things such as petrol and oil, but usually also provide toilets and sell food, drink and other goods
6 A point on a motorway where traffic may leave or join it
7 A word that means 'a complete stop of movement'
8 A word that is short for 'representative'
9 A word that refers to activities that people carry out over a period of time in order to achieve something such as social, political or commercial change

Exam tip

The language that writers use in texts depends on the readers that they expect. For example, in blogs, you will find informal language, whereas in journal articles you would find formal language. In very informal texts you may also find capitalizations, emoticons (smileys) and exclamations marks (LIKE THIS ☺ !). In order to understand texts better, ask yourself what sort of language is being used and who the intended readers of the text are.

4 **Copy and complete the table. Divide the following items into two categories: formal (or neutral) or informal.**

| to be fed up | to commute | almost | pretty much | a rep |
| a campaign | guys | options | anger | a junction |

Formal or neutral	Informal

5 **Match the following sentences with the type of text they have most likely been taken from.**

1 Nowadays, there is increasing traffic on our roads.   a newspaper article
2 The current traffic problems will be analysed with the aid of practical models.   b academic journal article
3 The traffic problems are getting ridiculous … ARGH!   c student essay
4 Traffic problems are bringing the UK to a standstill, road organizations have claimed.   d personal email

Exam information | Yes/No/Not Given

In the exam, you may be asked to demonstrate that you understand the points of view expressed in a text. You will be given a list of statements which each represents an opinion. You have to read the text to find out if the writer expresses these opinions or not. If the writer shares the opinion in the statement, your answer will be YES. If the writer contradicts the statement, your answer will be NO. If it is impossible to know from the text what the writer's opinion is about that subject, your answer will be NOT GIVEN.

The information in the text will be in the same order as the list of statements.

1 **It is important to understand the difference between facts and opinions. An opinion does not have to be based on fact or knowledge and we cannot prove it right or wrong.**
Are the following statements facts or opinions?

1 The distance between Birmingham and Cheltenham is about 40 miles. ....

2 There are currently two areas with roadworks between Birmingham and Cheltenham. ....

3 Cheltenham has music, literature and horseracing festivals, a historic promenade and award-winning gardens. ....

4 Cheltenham is well worth a visit. ....

5 Birmingham is sometimes compared to Venice because of its many canals. ....

6 You can't get from Birmingham to Cheltenham in less than half an hour unless you break the speed limit. ....

7 Frankley service station, on the M5 near Birmingham, has shops that provide good value for money. ....

2a **Read the texts and the statements that follow them. Write YES if the opinion is expressed in the text (=the writer agrees) and NO if the writer disagrees.**

Britain never used to have armed police, but when major events are being held, such as the recent London Olympics, there is a visible presence of armed police in train stations. Do people using public transport feel reassured when they see armed police? Possibly. But most of them, especially visitors to the UK, may feel that there is something to worry about, especially as they would expect British police not to be armed. And if we think about it, the police, armed or not, cannot protect us from bombers. But what the police can, and sometimes does do, is make mistakes, and these are always worse when there are firearms involved. So in the end, arming police may do more harm than good.

1 Most travellers feel protected when they see armed police in train stations. ....

2 Even police with guns cannot protect us from bombers. ....

3 The police might shoot somebody by accident. ....

4 It is better not to have armed police in Britain. ....

Instead of complaining about roadworks, the cost of petrol, the price of cars, etc. we need to think about other options. And I don't mean car sharing or building more motorways. I say we try to save our environment by campaigning for better bus and train networks and for different types of transport, such as trams.

5 We should complain about car-related problems. ....

6 The environment is not really in danger. ....

7 Public transport needs to be improved. ....

The rise in fuel prices is a very worrying trend. Here are just some examples of the consequences.

Elderly people cannot afford to heat their houses, people lose their jobs because they can no longer afford to commute to work, or because they are made redundant from their jobs in transport-based businesses such as airlines. Self-employed people often rely on their own transport for work, e.g. delivery people, florists and taxi drivers, so they may be forced to close their business. The prices of some food and raw materials also increase as a direct result of the cost of oil, e.g. the prices of beef and cotton. Against all of that, there is one possible advantage: car manufacturers are employing more people to design fuel-efficient cars, which will benefit the environment. But surely, this is not enough. What we need is international cooperation and political goodwill, to reduce fuel prices and/or financially support those who are being affected.

8 We need to be concerned about the increase in the price of fuel. ....

9 There are more problems caused by increasing fuel prices than the ones mentioned in the passage. ....

10 The price of beef is closely related to the price of oil. ....

11 The rise of fuel prices is not a big problem as the environment is benefitting from it. ....

12 If we cannot lower the price of fuel then we need more money so that people can cope with it. ....

2b Notice how synonyms and paraphrases were often used in the statements. For each statement in exercise 2a, underline the word(s) in the text that helped you.

Exam tip

To help you determine if something is NOT GIVEN, look for synonyms and paraphrases. If none appear, the answer will probably be NOT GIVEN. But even if you do find paraphrases, be careful: it may be that the topic is mentioned but not in relation to the statement.

3 Look back at the third passage in exercise 2a. Are the following opinions in the text (✓) or are they NOT GIVEN?

1 Old people may die because they cannot keep warm. ....

2 There is more unemployment when fuel prices rise. ....

3 People who deliver goods may use their personal vehicles to do this. ....

4 The price of corn and corn-based foods are related to the price of oil. ....

5 There already exist some fuel-efficient cars. ....

6 Politicians are not working hard enough now to solve fuel price problems. ....

Exam tip

Throughout the exam, you need to make sure you rely on the information in the passages, not on your own ideas. This is especially important with this type of question: never be tempted to reflect your own opinion, always consider only what is in the text.

Questions 1–12

Read the following passage. Do the statements agree with the views of the writer? Write:

YES   if the statement agrees with the views of the writer

NO   if the statement contradicts what the writer thinks

NOT GIVEN   if it is impossible to know what the writer's point of view is

1 Another name for the East-West trading route is 'silk road'. ....

2 Zhang Qian is admired by Chinese schoolchildren. ....

3 Zhang Qian was a Chinese adventurer. ....

4 At least one German used the silk road in the 19th century. ....

5 Silk was the main material to be traded on this route. ....

6 The silk road was used for trade in natural materials, man-made materials and animals. ....

7 We know that Zhang Qian was the first person to use the silk road. ....

8 The Romans may well have used the silk road. ....

9 The reports about a 'stone tower' provide evidence that the Romans used the silk road. ....

10 Kashgar is a welcoming city. ....

11 People who go in the Taklaman desert never come back out. ....

12 The journey from West to East was so long and difficult that the travellers probably did not go all the way to China. ....

Schoolchildren in China learn that the opening of the East-West trading route popularly known as the silk road occurred in 139 B.C. when Zhang Qian, the Chinese ambassador-adventurer, travelled westward across the Pamirs, a mountain range in Central Asia. He was the first known Chinese person to do so. The term 'silk road' was actually first used late in the nineteenth century by a German geographer, Baron Ferdinand von Richthofen (1833–1905). Silk was not the only material that passed along these routes. Other goods are known to have included ceramics, glass, precious gems and livestock.

However, there are reasons to think that these roads were being used centuries, probably even millennia, earlier than Zhang's expedition. In Roman times, Pliny the Elder reported a 'stone tower' which he said existed on the Pamir Plateau where goods had been traditionally exchanged between traders from the East and the West. In the early second century, Maës Titianus, an ancient Roman-Macedonian traveller, actually reported reaching this famous Stone Tower, but its exact location remains uncertain. According to one theory, it was at Tashkurgan in the Pamirs. (The word 'Tashkurgan' actually means 'stone tower' or 'stone fortress' in the Uyghur language.) Scholars today, however, believe that its location was probably somewhere in the Alay Valley. Whatever the truth about the Stone Tower may be, it seems likely that that some form trade was taking place in this region millennia before more formal recorded trade took place.

On the other hand, it is difficult to believe that people in those times were able to travel such huge distances. Travelling from West to East, the trader first had to cross the Pamir Plateau, through the 20,000-foot-high mountains. If the weather in the mountains had been kind and the journey undertaken in the right season, the eastward bound traveller would then finally arrive at the Kashgar, a logical place for trade and rest, where they could exchange horses or camels and then start on the return journey back over the mountains before the winter snows started.

It is unlikely that in these earlier times traders or travellers would have continued further eastwards from Kashgar, as they would have had to go round the Taklamakan Desert. Going through it was not an option as its name suggests: it literally means 'Go in and you won't come out'. Beyond this desert, there still would have remained eight hundred miles of a dangerous journey before they would have found the first true signs of Chinese civilization.

Adapted from The Moon over Matsushima - Insights into Mugwort and Moxa, by Merlin Young (Godiva Press).

Progress check

How many boxes can you tick? You should work towards being able to tick them all.

Did you …

remember that the questions are in the same order as the information in the text? ☐

base your answers on the text, not on your own opinion? ☐

look for synonyms and paraphrases in the text? ☐

focus on detail to make sure that the information in the statement related to exactly what was in the passage? ☐

Review 4

1   Answer or think about the following questions about units 10–12.

    1   What was your favourite topic from units 10–12?

    2   What was the best exam tip you read in these units?

    3   What crime-related vocabulary can you remember from unit 11?

    4   Can you explain the difference between Great Britain and England?

    5   Which profession would you prefer to have: SOCO, police officer, London bus driver, primary school teacher? Why?

    6   Has there been any change in how confident you feel about the IELTS reading exam?

2   Write the adjectives for each of these words. If you don't remember, you can look back at unit 10.

    1   administration ....

    2   day ....

    3   tradition ....

    4   Cornwall ....

    5   Britain ....

    6   geography ....

    7   Victoria ....

    8   Edward ....

    9   George ....

3   Can you remember the crime-related idioms from unit 11 that include these nouns?

nose	wrist	music	board	murder	robbery

4   In the paragraphs below, underline all the facts and highlight the opinions.

Beaumaris castle is an impressive medieval castle. It was built by King Edward I and is considered one of the most beautiful Edwardian castles in Wales, probably because of its symmetrical shapes, but its purpose was military. Work started in 1295, but although it was done at a fast speed, it was never completed because of lack of money.

Scotland is right to be proud of Edinburgh castle. It dominates the city of Edinburgh from high up on its rock. The history of Castle Rock goes back all the way to the late Bronze Age (900 BC), when there were already people living there. It is now mainly known as a visitor attraction. Although it is more expensive than other tourist attractions, people visit it because it offers excellent value.

5   Choose the correct heading for each of the paragraphs A–D from this list. You will not use them all.

    i   Making CCTV effective

    ii   Is CCTV really effective?

    iii   How CCTV works

    iv   Crime fighting with technology

    v   The fight against terrorism

    vi   The use of CCTV cameras

    vii   The police and their opinion

A ....

Crime-fighting technology is getting more sophisticated and rightly so. The police need to be equipped for the 21st century. In Britain we've already got the world's biggest DNA database. By next year the state will have access to the genetic data of 4.25m people: one British-based person in 14. Hundreds of thousands of those on the database will never have been charged with a crime.

B ....

Britain is also reported to have more than 4 million CCTV (closed circuit television) cameras. There is a continuing debate about the effectiveness of CCTV. Some evidence suggests that it is helpful in reducing shoplifting and car crime. It has also been used to successfully identify terrorists and murderers.

C ....

However, many claim that better lighting is just as effective to prevent crime and that cameras could displace crime. An internal police report said that only one crime was solved for every 1,000 cameras in London in 2007. In short, there is conflicting evidence about the effectiveness of cameras, so it is likely that the debate will continue.

D ....

Professor Mike Press, who has spent the past decade studying how design can contribute to crime reduction, said that, in order for CCTV to have any effect, it must be used in a targeted way.

6   **Read the following passage. Do the statements agree with the views of the writer? Write:**

YES   if the statement agrees with the claims of the writer,
NO   if the statement contradicts the writer's claims,
NOT GIVEN   if it is impossible to know what the writer thinks about this.

Text	Statements	YES/NO/ NOT GIVEN
Despite Victorian times being characterized by romanticism, the famous British romantic poets belong to the period before Queen Victoria.	1 The romantic poets are not normally described as Victorian poets.	
From the same era date famous writers such as Jane Austen and Mary Shelley (who wrote Frankenstein), and great architects such as James Wyatt and John Nash.	2 Jane Austen and Mary Shelly were two authors who knew each other well.	
And, even if we know they can all be described as Georgian artists, which King George does this refer to? Actually, it refers to four of them (George I, George II, George III and George IV), and thus spans a long period incorporating most of the 18th century and some of the 19th.	3 The adjective 'Georgian' can refer to people who lived during the period that King George I ruled.	
The Georgian style incorporates previous styles, including gothic, and has its own subdivision, Regency style, which describes the period of George IV.	4 The gothic style came after the Georgian style.	
	5 George IV was a king who was known for his sense of style.	

Practice test

On pages 88–97 you will find an example of what the IELTS Reading exam looks like. Taking this practice test under timed conditions will give you an idea of what it will be like to take the actual exam.

You have one hour to complete the exam. This includes the time required to write your answers on an answer sheet. There are three passages, so aim to spend about twenty minutes on each of them.

Exam tip

Read the instructions carefully. They may be similar to what you have practised before, but maybe not exactly the same.

Read the first task before you start to read each passage so you know how to approach it.

Skip any questions you are not sure about, rather than wasting too much time on a particular question. You can come back to the missing answers later.

Remember to answer all the questions using information from the passages. Whether or not you are knowledgeable about the topic should not make any difference to your answers.

Do not leave answers blank if you run out of time: guess the answers where you can, as there is a chance you will get some right. This is especially true for multiple-choice questions, matching exercises and other questions where you have limited answer options.

READING PASSAGE 1

You should spend about 20 minutes on questions 1–14 which are based on Reading passage 1 below.

Is this the end of the High Street?

Take a walk down any 'High Street', normally places full of shops, and you'll notice signs that all is not well: they will say 'To Let'.

The High Street faces real competition from out-of-town retail parks and the steady growth of supermarkets, both in number and in size. There is also the growing trend for people to shop online, combined with a reduction in many families' finances which has affected customer confidence.

Retailing (the sale of goods from a fixed location) is changing too: shopping is becoming a leisure activity as much as a necessity, along with the rise of home delivery services saving time and journeys. Convenience is a powerful motivator for shoppers' behaviour. Is the traditional High Street dying out?

During the last two years, independent retailers have struggled more than the chain stores. Research suggests over 12,000 independent stores closed in 2009. Economies of scale (it is cheaper to buy stock in bulk, so big shops can charge lower prices) are one part of the issue.

Supermarkets have a stronger control over the supply chain and can manipulate prices more effectively. As a result of the decline in smaller stores, there are now many empty shops in most town centres, some of which have been vacant for some time, and have whitewashed windows. What impact do they have on the overall 'feel' of the town for visitors and residents?

More importantly, how does the loss of a familiar shop which has perhaps served decades of local residents affect people at a time when so many other familiar aspects of daily life are under threat? When a shopping mall is being planned, it is very important to secure the key 'anchor' tenants: the big names that can guarantee customers through the doors. Is the disappearance of these familiar local shops and small department stores like losing a link with the past?

The growth of CCTV cameras, use of private security firms and blurring of public and private land has also been an issue in cities such as Exeter. This can result in young people feeling that they are being victimized and forced out of city centres.

Another feature of many city centres is that they are beginning to look very similar to each other. The New Economics Foundation introduced the term 'clone town' in a report published in 2004. This suggests that many High Streets have few individual characteristics – the same shops can be seen in most towns. This was also followed up by a report in 2010, which identified Cambridge as the most 'cloned' city in the UK: one with very few independent stores in the centre.

Vacant shops are another issue for town centres. These can end up as charity shops, 'pop-up' shops (especially around Christmas) or attract vandals and graffiti. Some cities such as Portsmouth have made an effort to revamp empty store-fronts to improve those areas where they are found. This is important for cities which attract large numbers of tourists, such as Bath, York and Chester.

Services are perhaps more resilient to these changes, particularly those that offer something that is not available online. As one person commented: 'You can't have your hair cut online …' – well, not yet anyway. This partly explains the growth of coffee shops and nail bars in some town centres, which are going against the general trend.

Finally, out on the edges of our towns, the supermarkets continue to grow – they've got the town centre surrounded. A report published in late 2010 said that around 55p of every £1 that we spend is spent in supermarkets, and there have been a large number of planning applications for further stores.

Glossary

the High Street: (British) the main street of a town, usually where the principal shops are situated

QUESTIONS 1–6

Do the following statements agree with the views of the writer? Write:

YES   if the statement agrees with the views of the writer
NO   if the statement contradicts what the writer thinks
NOT GIVEN   if it is impossible to know what the writer's point of view is

1 Not only are supermarkets getting bigger, there are more of them than ever.
....

2 People have less money now, so they try to buy cheaper goods via the Internet.
....

3 People shop because they have to, but also because it is fun. ....

4 The younger generation may feel unwelcome in certain towns. ....

5 Although most towns have the same shops, there are many features that make them unique. ....

6 Although a large number of stores are closing, the number of shops that offer services is increasing. ....

QUESTIONS 7–10

Look at the following features (7–10) and the list of groups below. Match each item with the correct group (A–D).

NB You may use any letter more than once.

7 there are fewer of them   ....

8 competition is increasing   ....

9 business is getting better   ....

10 are often located outside of the city centre   ....

This is true for:

     A independent shops that sell goods

     B supermarkets

     C both supermarkets and independent shops

     D private security firms

QUESTIONS 11–14

Choose the appropriate letters a–d to finish sentences 11–14.

11 Britain's High Streets are
   a   full of shops.
   b   suffering because of online shopping.
   c   convenient for shoppers.
   d   providing more competition for chain stores.

12 Economies of scale
   a   are causing problems for independent shops.
   b   means that bigger shops can buy more goods.
   c   affected 12,000 independent stores in 2009.
   d   are responsible for the economic problems of the past two years.

13 Shopping malls
   a   are being built in High Streets.
   b   are increasingly using CCTV.
   c   are being planned in Cambridge.
   d   like having well-known shops.

14 Nail bars
   a   are no longer trendy.
   b   are becoming more popular.
   c   are starting to offer online services.
   d   are also starting to cut hair.

11 .... 12 .... 13 .... 14 ....

READING PASSAGE 2

You should spend about 20 minutes on questions 15–27 which are based on Reading passage 2 below.

London's cycle hire scheme

A London is a 'world city': one of the most important economic and financial hubs in the world. It has a population of around eight million people and contains hundreds of iconic buildings which are recognized the world over. London receives around 20 million visitors each year, a large proportion from overseas, who mingle with further millions of people who travel into the city from a wide area to work in the central area. It is frequently rated as providing the most satisfying 'cultural experience' for visitors to any city.

B One of the challenges involved in managing (and living in) such a huge city is the ability to move people efficiently around it, for the purposes of work and leisure, and at reasonable cost. The London black cab is one response to this problem, but it also contributes to the number of vehicles that are on the roads. The much quoted result of millions of daily vehicle movements is a very low average speed for traffic on London's roads and frequent congestion problems.

C Many cities have taken steps to reduce the amount of traffic on the roads by adopting a range of measures which can broadly be described as either 'carrots' or 'sticks': those which either promote, or discourage certain activity. London has already been forced into trying a number of measures to reduce traffic congestion. These have included:

- Traffic management systems which included the world's first traffic light. It was installed outside the Houses of Parliament in 1868 to reduce congestion in this area.

- An underground system which was the first in the world. The first section opened in 1863, and the network is still developing. Since 2003, it has been managed by Transport for London. The classic London Tube map forms part of the city's cultural heritage, and has been much copied and adapted elsewhere.

- The Cross Rail development: due to provide high frequency rail services through two new tunnels under Central London from 2017.

- The congestion charging system – introduced in 2003, and extended in 2007 – charges many motorists (there are some exemptions) £10 to enter the central charging zone between 7 a.m.–6 p.m. Monday to Friday.

- The Oyster card – an automated charging system which speeds up the use of public transport using a specially chipped card, which can be pre-charged with 'credit'.

D The latest solution is the Barclays London Cycle Hire Scheme. In 2010, London joined a growing list of cities that had turned to the bicycle for a possible solution to traffic congestion. Cities like Amsterdam have long since been associated with bicycles. Other cities that already have cycle hire schemes include Copenhagen and Barcelona. In Paris, the system is known as the Velib scheme, a word which merges the word for *bicycle* with *freedom*. It is funded by advertising. The London scheme was launched on the 30th July 2010 with an initial total of 5,000 bikes spread around 315 locations, with plans for further extensions. The bikes are fairly robust so that they can withstand the knocks of daily use. They are fitted with dynamo-powered LED lights, have three gears, a chain guard and a bell. Each bike is also fitted with a Radio Frequency Identification (RFID) chip, so that its location can be tracked. The bikes have puncture-proof tyres and are regularly checked over for mechanical faults.

E   It is hoped that people will experience London in a more direct way. Instead of descending into the earth, they will cycle the streets and thus gain 'a different view' of London and improve their own mental maps of the city. They will also be getting exercise, which in an age of soaring obesity rates can only be a good thing, can't it?

Enough reading, time for you to get out there and start pedalling!

Glossary

the Tube: the underground railway system in London

QUESTIONS 15–18

Choose one of the endings (i–viii) from the List of Endings to complete each sentence below. The information in the completed sentences should accurately reflect what is said in the text.

NB There are more endings (i–viii) than sentence beginnings, so you will not need to use them all. You may use each ending once only.

15 London … ………

16 London traffic … ………

17 The London Cycle hire scheme … ………

18 The London underground … ………

List of endings

    i has influenced others.

    ii has twenty millions foreign visitors a year.

    iii is not an original idea.

    iv is a place where travellers can feel safe.

    v is not organized as well as it is elsewhere.

    vi is slow.

    vii has had to try and solve traffic problems.

    viii causes pollution.

QUESTIONS 19–23

Reading passage 2 has five sections, A–E.

Choose the most suitable headings for sections A–E from the list of headings below. Write the appropriate numbers (i–ix) next to the sections.

NB There are more headings than sections, so you will not use them all.

List of headings

    i Current and past actions

    ii Congestion and pollution

    iii Problems on the roads

    iv The best city in the world

    v A centre of activity

    vi The many benefits of cycling

    vii Cycling in European cities

    viii A new initiative

    ix Rail systems

19 Section A ....

20 Section B ....

21 Section C ....

22 Section D ....

23 Section E ....

QUESTIONS 24–27

Complete the summary below, each time with **ONE WORD** from Reading passage 2.

The Barclays London Cycle Hire Scheme was started in 2010 in the hope of providing a (24) .... for the existing transport issues. The money that was necessary to have a scheme like this was sourced from (25) .... and allowed London to have 5,000 bikes initially, but there are likely to be (26) .... to the scheme. The bikes have a tracking (27) ...., are properly equipped and regularly maintained.

READING PASSAGE 3

You should spend about 20 minutes on questions 28–40 which are based on Reading passage 3 below.

Personalized exercise

A   At the start of every new year, many of us promise ourselves that a certain number of times a week we will go to the gym, go jogging, attend an exercise class, etc. But many of us struggle to fit exercise into our lives, or we start off well and then give up.

B   The key could be to find the right type of exercise for you. After all, if we end up doing something we enjoy and can see the benefits of, we are more likely to carry on for longer than a few weeks. Studies suggest that six weeks are all it takes to form a habit, so once we have managed to continue for that length of time, chances are that exercise has become a routine part of our lives that we do not question. So what exercise is right for you? Read on to find out.

C   First of all, you need to determine your motivation. Are you mainly interested in de-stressing or in getting fitter? If your ultimate goal is relaxation, then ask yourself if you want to do this energetically, in which case a type of martial art or exercise based on boxing may be right for you. If you have a calmer style, then you could choose solitary exercise, such as walking the dog, doing some gardening, or opting for a brisk daily walk around the block. If you get more motivated from working with others, then you could join a yoga, pilates or t'ai chi class, all designed to stretch and strengthen your muscles and with the added benefit of calming the mind.

D   If it is fitness and weight loss you are after, then group activities include military fitness, typically organized in local parks, walking and running groups, dance classes (try line dancing, tap dancing or ballet). Contact your local council for details of those. On your own, you could go horse riding, swimming, or if you fear that you will choose not to leave your house, download fitness and motivational exercise programmes that you can do at home.

E   Finally, even people who are incredibly busy have no excuse. It is getting easier to fit exercise into our lives, rather than having to make so many changes to our lifestyles that we are doomed to fail. If you have particular time slots available, then you could book some time with a personal trainer at the weekend who can come to your house, or you could meet them at the gym. During the week, you could use the daily commute for your exercise, by walking faster, parking the car further away from work, or getting your bicycle out. If your life is not as regular, you could choose the next couple of minutes you have spare to try an exercise DVD, or get the skipping ropes out and do some skipping. You could also go outdoors to your nearest fitness trail, or put your running shoes on and run for any length of time, as everything counts when you are doing exercise.

F   You see? There is no excuse. Whatever your lifestyle, you will be able to find something that suits you. Just sit down with a cup of tea, read this article again, have a think about your options. Then finish the tea, get up, get going, and don't stop.

Use NO MORE THAN THREE WORDS from the passage to complete each blank in the diagram below.

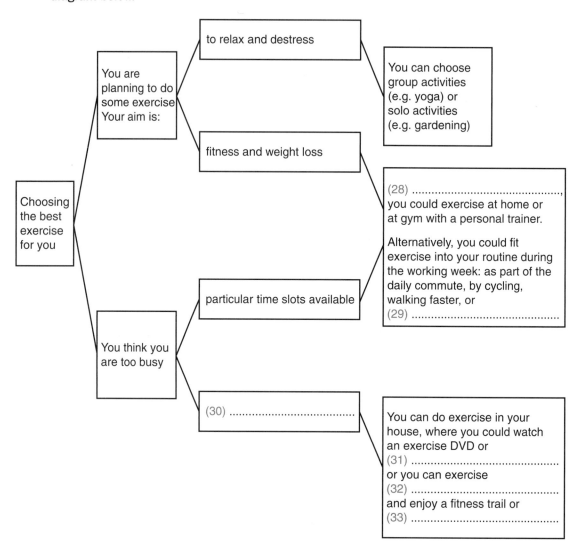

Choosing the best exercise for you

You are planning to do some exercise Your aim is:

to relax and destress

You can choose group activities (e.g. yoga) or solo activities (e.g. gardening)

fitness and weight loss

(28) ...., you could exercise at home or at gym with a personal trainer.

Alternatively, you could fit exercise into your routine during the working week: as part of the daily commute, by cycling, walking faster, or (29) ....

You think you are too busy

particular time slots available

(30) ....

You can do exercise in your house, where you could watch an exercise DVD or (31) .... or you can exercise (32) .... and enjoy a fitness trail or (33) ....

QUESTIONS 34–36

Reading passage 3 has six paragraphs A–F. Which paragraphs state the following information? Write the appropriate letters A–F next to numbers 34–36.

NB There are more paragraphs than summaries, so you will not use them all.

34 It is recommendable to take action without delay. ....

35 Suitable exercise is more long term. ....

36 Get fitter wherever you are. ....

QUESTIONS 37–38

Using **NO MORE THAN THREE WORDS** from the text for each, answer the following questions.

37 What kind of activity do people who would rather exercise alone prefer?

....

38 Who can provide information about organized sports or fitness activities with others?

....

QUESTIONS 39–40

Do the following statements agree with the information in the passage? Write:

TRUE   if the text confirms the statement
FALSE   if the text contradicts of the statement
NOT GIVEN   if it is impossible to know from the text

39 It is important to try and exercise for six weeks without giving up. ....

40 Having a cup of tea is part of a healthy lifestyle. ....

Answer key

Unit 1   Friendship

Part 1   Vocabulary

Exercise 1a
2 sharing
3 having fun
4 chatting

Exercise 1b
1 sharing
2 Partying
3 Chatting
4 having fun

Exercise 2

play	go	do
chess	swimming	sports
basketball	dancing	weightlifting
board games	skiing	yoga
sports	shopping	exercise
tennis	hiking	karate
cards		puzzles
poker		kick boxing

1 go
2 play
3 do

Exercise 3a
Jack, 15: I spend time with my family most evenings. At the weekend, I prefer to hang out with my friends at the park or in the playground in the local woods. If it rains, I like to go to see a film with my friends.
Monica, 18: I belong to a chess club which meets twice a month, and once a year we go camping. It's the highlight of my summer! We stay in tents on a lovely camp site and have picnics and barbecues. In the evenings, we organize quizzes and play cards. And we also play a lot of chess, of course!

Amrita, 12: My older sisters spend a lot of time with their friends in the local shopping centre, but I'm not allowed to go out without an adult yet. I can still chat to my friends all the time though, by phone, email or text message.

Exercise 3b
1 shopping centre
2 an adult
3 a camp site
4 a picnic
5 barbecues (singular: a barbecue)
6 quizzes (singular: a quiz)

Part 2   Skills development

Exercise 3
Suggested answers:
1 Why are Ben, Rory and Carlos mentioned in the article?
2 Which of the following best describes Ben?
3 What do we know about the lake that Rory visits?
4 Carlos mentions that he is left-handed because …
5 The answers to the recent research and the answers from the readers…

Exercise 4
i   The correct answer is b – It is true what is said in d: they are teenage boys, but they are mentioned because what they said about themselves is part of the article (b). c says that they read magazines, but we only know that they are readers of the magazine that the text was in, not that they read magazines in general, and in any case this would not be enough of a reason for them to appear in this magazine. a is not correct: they say why *they* value friendship, but we don't know if this is true about all teenagers.

ii The correct answer is d – we know he likes football and skateboarding. It is true that he has fights with his parents sometimes (a), but we don't know that he often fights, or that he fights with other people. b says that he generally likes to be alone, but we only know that that is true after he has had a fight with his parents. We have no information about c because we don't know how happy he and his friends are.

iii The correct answer is b – when people say something is nearby, without saying near what, they mean near their house. It may be in a village (d) or near the school (a) too, but we cannot be sure. As Rory uses the lake for water sports, it is likely that other people do too, but the text does not tell us that *a lot of people do* (c).

iv The correct answer is b – we have no information about a or d. It may be an interesting fact (c) but there is a reason why he mentions it: his friends had to copy his notes for him. This is because he is left-handed and uses his left hand for writing: being left-handed made the situation more difficult for him (b).

v The correct answer is c – a is incorrect: the article says the results were not really surprising. Although sports were mentioned, d is incorrect because the results were about what teenagers say is important to them. The results were not exactly the same (b), but they were similar (c) because some aspects of them were the same: the research said that *they value friendship above everything else*; the readers said that *they value friendship very highly*.

Part 3   Exam practice

i a
30 real friends or fewer (a) is the same as *no more than 30 friends*. b means 30 friends or more. It is true that most internet users have about 150 friends (c) but it does not say anywhere that the majority of people are internet users. The number 400 refers to real friends, not internet friends (d).

ii d
Friendship means different things in different situations (the end of the first paragraph) means that a definition of friendship is difficult: it depends on the situation. The other items are not correct. The following are mentioned: *the numbers* (a), *keeping friends* (not: keeping them *happy* (b)) and *social networking sites* (c). However, the specific statements are not true.

iii a
The paragraph describes the different views that people have about friendship. The other topics are mentioned but what is said about them is not in the text.

iv c
In the text, *we fear we have left it too late in life to start*, corresponds to *they worry because they think they are too old*. b is not mentioned. People may have many friends (a) but this is not something that is described as a worry. d is true, and it may lead to problems, but again, this is not described as something that people worry about.

v d
Something that is *shared by many* is something that people have in common. Here this refers to *the need to be around other people* (d). The dissatisfaction refers to the different meanings of friendship, not to friends themselves (a). b and c may be true, but there is no evidence of that in the text.

vi d
d is the correct answer as the text refers to *strangers* where it says *people who in the future may become our friends*. We could say that a is true and b is false, as the definition of 'stranger' is *a person we have not met before*. However, this is not mentioned in the text. c is often said, but again there is no evidence of this in the text. It is important

that your answer reflects what is said in the text, so don't rely on your general knowledge or opinion.

Unit 2   Body and mind

Part 1   Vocabulary

Exercise 1a
1 club
2 racket
3 bat
4 board

Exercise 1b
Possible answers:
snowboarding, skateboarding, surfing, bodyboarding, windsurfing, snow kiting, kitesurfing

Exercise 1c
1 golf
2 badminton
3 windsurfing
4 cricket

Exercise 2
positive feelings: amazed, amused, calm, confident, curious, delighted, excited, glad, happy, relaxed, wonderful
negative feelings: afraid, angry, annoyed, anxious, ashamed, bored, depressed, disappointed, embarrassed, frightened, guilty, jealous, miserable, nervous, sad, terrible, tired

Exercise 3
There are a number of possible answers, but they must have the underlined endings:
1 tired
2 amus<u>ing</u>
3 embarrass<u>ing</u>
4 relaxed
5 depress<u>ing</u>
6 excit<u>ing</u>
7 amus<u>ing</u>
8 frighten<u>ed</u>

Part 2   Skills development

Exercise 1
1 nine
2 ten
3 eleven
4 thirteen

Exercise 2
Suggested answers:
2 during pregnancy
3 he needs medication
4 (no change necessary)

Exercise 3
Possible answers:
1 regular exercise (2 words)
2 I love it (3 words)
3 reading, watching films (3 words)
4 to keep fit (3 words)

Exercise 4
The following wouldn't help:
reading the text before reading the questions; underlining the key words in the text.

Exercise 5
Suggested answers:
1 <u>Why</u> do <u>some people</u> <u>accept</u> <u>pain</u> as a <u>part of life</u>?
2 <u>What</u> did <u>Blaxter</u> <u>want</u> to <u>find out</u> about?
3 What does the text say about <u>how</u> <u>older people</u> <u>define</u> <u>health</u>?

Exercise 6
Suggested answers:
1 they are older
2 health definitions
3 ability to cope

Part 3   Exam practice
Suggested answers:
 i shapes, heights, colours, abilities
 ii genetics, ageing social factors
 iii physically difficult or inactive

iv housing (conditions) and neighbourhoods
v culture and media
vi the idea of slimness / ideal body shape
vii belly or stomach
vii biologically and socially
ix exercise and food
x wrong and unhealthy

Unit 3   Studying abroad

Part 1   Vocabulary

Exercise 1a
1 c
2 d
3 a
4 b

Exercise 1b
1 RE (<u>R</u>eligious <u>E</u>ducation)
2 numeracy
3 PE (<u>P</u>hysical <u>E</u>ducation)
4 literacy

Exercise 2
1 nursery school
2 infant school
3 primary school
4 secondary school
5 6th form college
6 bachelor's degree
7 master's degree
8 PhD

Exercise 3
1 Vietnam
2 Hanoi
3 Japan
4 Kyoto
5 Arabic
6 Arab
7 Jeddah
8 German
9 Heidelberg
10 Dutch
11 Maastricht
12 Dutch
13 Brussels
14 German
15 Zurich

Exercise 4
1 remember
2 remember
3 reminds
4 remember
5 Remind

Part 2   Skills development

Exercise 1
Paragraph numbers 2 and 3

Exercise 2

Countries	People	Organizations or institutions
Australia	Russel Howe	the British Council
the UK	Manal	Stellinga International
the US	the faculty	College
Germany	of Art and	
China	design (at	
Malaysia	Stellinga)	
Japan		
Russia		
Nigeria		
Brazil		
the Netherlands		
India		
(note: Europe is not a country)		

Exercise 3

numbers	10, one, two, 5, 11th, 1
words in italics	needed, wanted internationalization
words in bold print	[the title and all subheadings]
abbreviations	UK, US, i.e., e.g.

Exercises 4 and 5

1 paragraphs 2 and 3 – the quotation marks help to find this answer.

2 that it was a choice (something he *wanted* to do), and not a necessity (something he *needed* to do). The italics make it clear that he wants to emphasize this.

3 paragraphs 1 and 4 – in the first paragraph, it mentions *most welcoming* and talks about Germany as the country at the top of the list. In paragraph 4, the uppercase letter of Germany, is easy to spot and the word *winner* appears very near.

4 paragraph 4 – *internationalization* is printed in italics.

Part 3   **Exam practice**

Suggested answers:

1 equivalent
2 International Baccalaureate
2 personal statement
4 1000 words
5 passport
6 translations
7 interview
8 on site
9 phone
10 successful
11 waiting list

Review 1

Exercise 1

There are, of course, different possibilities, but here are some examples of right and wrong answers. Notice how some of the ones on the left are like sentences, whereas the ones on the right use more nouns and are like titles.

wrong (too long)	right
1 chicken, rice and peas	chicken and rice
2 I went to work	office work
3 meeting my wonderful wife	meeting my wife
4 do what you think is best for you	follow your dreams
5 travelling around the whole world on a luxury boat	a world cruise
6 getting a high enough IELTS score to study in the UK	passing IELTS *OR* studying abroad

Exercise 2

1 j – You can spend time and you can spend money (see f), but sentence f does not match grammatically.
2 g – You can play sports and musical instruments (see h), but sentence h does not match grammatically. Adults do not 'play' with their friends (see l).
3 k
4 h
5 a – You could also live near the woods (see i) but you wouldn't just live there in your spare time.
6 d
7 c
8 f – Sentence ending e is not correct because of the extra 'that'.

Exercise 3

1 charge fees
2 take a class
3 keep in touch
4 have fun
5 value friendship
6 play cards
7 study abroad

Exercise 4

Suggested answers:
1 I can't think of anything more **boring** than a picnic in the park.
2 Have you reminded her that it starts at half past eight? [*correct*]
3 When I have no college work, I usually go to my friends to play **cards/ computer games/ sports** ...
4 Can you **remind** me that I need to do some washing?
5 I have never felt so sad and **depressed** in my life.
6 **Partying** with friends is my favourite activity.
7 I am very **excited** to see you.
8 There is no need to be embarrassed, just come in. [*correct*]

Exercise 5

Possible answers:
1 bored, tired
2 depressed, disappointed, bored, worried, annoyed
3 frightened, surprised, scared, shocked
4 excited, delighted, amazed
5 relaxed, tired, satisfied

Exercise 6

1 literacy
2 numeracy
3 student
4 university
5 degree
6 research
7 diploma
8 application

Unit 4 Science and technology at home

Part 1 Vocabulary

Exercise 1a

1 measuring jug
2 flask
3 kettle
4 kitchen scales

Exercise 1b

1 kettle
2 flask
3 kitchen scales
4 measuring jug

Exercise 2a

2 a	5 f	8 j
3 h	6 c	9 d
4 b	7 e	10 i

Exercise 2b

Suggested answers:

1 *a biography*: a book / story about another person's life
2 *an autobiography*: a book you write about yourself / written by the author about their own life

Part 2 Skills development

Exercise 1

1 d	4 g	7 e
2 a	5 c	
3 b	6 f	

Exercise 2

1 d	3 e	5 f
2 a	4 c	6 b

Exercise 3

2 There are some <u>materials that allow electricity to pass through them</u>. These <u>electrical conductors</u> are used in many different appliances in the home.

3 Another example is <u>electrical insulators, substances that do not let electricity pass through</u>.

4 We sell any computer you can imagine, from the traditional desktop to <u>tablet computers</u> and other kinds of <u>mobile computers</u>, as well as cameras and e-readers.

5 Your smartphone's <u>operating system</u> may be the same or a different <u>OS</u> to the one controlling your tablet.

Exercise 4

Mobile phone components [1 parts]
An average [2 typical] basic mobile phone contains a circuit board, an antenna, a liquid crystal [3] display, a keyboard, a microphone, a speaker and a battery.

Mobile metals
Mobiles contain [4 include] many different metals:

- Copper is used for electrical circuits [5] because it is a good electrical conductor.
- Silver is used in switches on the circuit boards and in the phone buttons because it is an even better electrical conductor. It lasts for millions [6 a very large amount] of on/off cycles.
- Gold is used to plate [7 coat] the surfaces of the circuit board and the connectors. It is an excellent [8 exceptional] electrical conductor and does not corrode [9].
- Tantalum is used in the electronic components. It enables scientists to make mobiles very small [10 tiny].

Your mobile is also likely to contain palladium, platinum, aluminium and iron.

Electrical conductivity
Metals conduct [11 transfer] electrical currents well. Non-metals usually make good insulators. In a mobile, electrical insulators surround [12] the circuit.

Smart mobiles

The next [13 following] generation of mobile could be made from 'smart' fabric [14 material]. These types of fabric react to something in the environment and change. A smart fabric mobile could be folded [15] and put in your pocket without breaking.

Part 3   Exam practice

 i chemical reaction
 ii separated (out)
 iii refuse
 iv source
 v identical

Unit 5   Back to nature

Part 1   Vocabulary

Exercise 1

1 waterfall
2 valley
3 bay
4 cliff

Exercise 2

1 land
2 sand
3 ground
4 soil

Exercise 3a

Suggested answers:

Our knowledge of Natural History would not be what it is today without the work of women explorers, artists and scientists. In this leaflet, you will learn about three British pioneering women, first to be involved in uncovering some of the rich history of the natural world.

Mary Anning (1799–1847)

Mary came from a poor family who lived in Lyme Regis, a coastal town in the South West of England. Her father tried to make extra money by selling fossils (remains in rocks) to rich tourists. Consequently, Mary and her siblings learned from an early age how to look for fossils, although she was the only one of the brothers and sisters who became an expert because she understood that fossils were of interest to geology and biology, not just tourism. However, in her lifetime she did not always get the credit she deserved, as it was male geologists who published the descriptions of any finds. Her important finds include the first skeleton of an ichthyosaur, or fish-lizard, a plesiosaur, also known as sea-dragon, and a pterodactyl, a 'flying dragon'.

Collecting fossils on the cliffs was dangerous work. Mary's dog Tray was killed when rocks and earth fell down a cliff, and she nearly lost her life in the same landslide, but in the end it was cancer that killed her when she was 47.

Dorothea Bate (1878–1951)

Born in the Welsh countryside, she had a passion for outdoor pursuits and natural history from an early age. She became the first female scientist in the Natural History museum in London. She was a palaeontologist, that is, a scientist who studies fossils in order to understand the history of life on Earth. She went to mountains and cliffs in the Mediterranean and explored hilltops in Bethlehem, discovering and documenting animal fossils. She wrote hundreds of reports, reviews and papers.

Evelyn Cheesman (1881–1969)

Although Evelyn wanted to become a veterinary surgeon, this was not possible for women in the early twentieth century. Instead, she trained as a canine nurse. Her first job, however, was not related to dogs: she worked in the insect house at the London Zoological society. She was very adventurous and went on many expeditions to remote locations, as far away as the Galapagos Islands. Despite being very busy, she managed to publish 16 books.

Exercise 3b
Lyme Regis – a coastal town in the South West of England
fossils – remains in rocks
siblings – brothers and sisters
ichthyosaur – fish-lizard
plesiosaur – sea-dragon
pterodactyl – flying dragon
Tray – Mary's dog
landslide – rocks and earth [falling] down a cliff
palaeontologist – scientist who studies fossils in order to understand the history of life on Earth
canine – related to dogs
remote – far away

Exercise 4
1 ✓ because there is a contrast between 'no evidence' and what people believe
2 ✗ because both sentences support the same information

Part 2   Skills development
Exercise 2
(Compare your drawing to the diagrams in exercise 3 to see if you included the main aspects.)

Exercise 3
1 mud, sand or soil
2 deeper (and deeper)
3 rock
4 (start to) crystallize
5 process
6 waves, tides and currents
7 break off

Part 3   Exam practice
1 drumsticks
2 (green) pods
3 green beans
4 nutrients

5 pickled/dried
6 dried/pickled
7 spinach
8 skin infections
9 joints
10 digestion
11 pleasant
12 milk flow
13 delicacy

Unit 6   Communication

Part 1   Vocabulary
Exercise 1
1 slogan
2 sign
3 logo
4 advertisement

Exercise 2a
Suggested answers:

It's impossible to avoid advertisements. In our homes, newspaper, magazine and television ads compete for our attention. Posters, billboards and flyers greet us the moment we walk out the door. Advertising agencies stay busy thinking up new ways to get our attention. We have company logos on our clothes. Our email is full of spam, and pop-ups slow us down as we surf the Web. Product placements sneak into films and TV shows. 'Ad wrapping' turns cars into moving signboards. Advertisers have even tried advertising in TV commercials in a subliminal way (affecting your mind without you knowing it). It's no wonder that this is called the consumer age.

1 spam
2 product placement
3 billboards
4 flyer
5 signboards
6 consumer
7 pop-up

Exercise 2b

2 magazine
3 television
4 advertising
5 company
6 product
7 TV
8 consumer

Exercise 3a

1 web
2 website
3 focus
4 individuals
5 corporation
6 comments
7 activity

Exercise 3b

1 A
2 an
3 a
4 the
5 the

Part 2 Skills development

Exercise 1

adjectives	nouns*	verbs	adverbs
mobile	satellite	transfer	fast
fast	newspaper	free	
free	mobile	signal	
speedy	transfer	access	
handy	broadband		
commercial	access		
	keyboard		
	consumer		
	commercial		
	signal		

* Note: these nouns can also be used in front of other nouns e.g. newspaper ad

Exercise 2

2 verb e.g. *return*
3 verb ending in *–ing,* e.g. *communicating;* verb ending in *–ed,* e.g. *communicated*
4 adjective (in comparative form) e.g. *better*
5 verb, e.g. *store;* adjective, e.g. *accurate* – (note that this is comparative form so *clear* would not be possible as the comparative form for one-syllable adjectives ends in *-er,* so it would be *clearer* not: *more clear*)
6 preposition: *into*

Exercise 3

The notes relate to the first part of the text, and the summary to the last part.

a
types of communication:
1 **spoken**
2 **written** } verbal
3 **non-verbal**

b
1 business
2 layout
3 mistakes
4 (annual) report
5 standard/predetermined

Part 3 Exam practice

Exercise 1

i relatively few speak a second language fluently
ii communication problems
iii effective written skills
iv customers, suppliers, trade union officials, government officials, the local community

Exercise 2

Summary A:
1 participants
2 plan
3 time
4 achieve
5 future

Summary B:
6 necessary
7 effective
8 employees
9 preventing

Review 2

Exercise 1
Check that you have used a maximum of five words.

Exercise 2
1 Although
2 For example
3 and
4 such as
5 also
6 However
7 in fact
(Note: you cannot start a sentence with *such as*)

Exercise 3
i – b
ii – a

Exercise 4
1 c – product placement
2 g – facial expression
3 h – public library
4 j – advertising agency
5 f – natural history
6 a – newspaper ad
7 b – coastal town
8 e – communication process
9 n – formal register
10 k – women explorers
11 d – outdoor pursuits
12 l – veterinary surgeon
13 i – financial information
14 m – marine animal

Exercise 5
1 fossil
2 seashells
3 jellyfish
4 tracks/footprints

Exercise 6
1 The secretary wrote the minutes of the meeting outlining the **agreements** we reached.
2 There are about 7 billion people in the world. ~~In fact,~~ About 1.3 billion of them live in China. (If you want to link these two sentences, you could say: *There are about 7 billion people in the world, about 1.3 billion of which live in China.*)
3 I always get **soil** (or *dirt/sand*) under my fingernails when I am gardening.
4 My **sister** (or *brother*] is the only sibling I have left.
5 Pickling and drying are methods of food preservation. [correct]

Unit 7 Business management

Part 1 Vocabulary

Exercise 1

1 b
2 e
3 d
4 a
5 i
6 h
7 g
8 c
9 f

Exercise 2a

Saving money	Borrowing money from the bank	Getting your own money from the bank	Earning money	Paying money
investment savings account	owe overdraft mortgage loan credit card	ATM withdrawal cash point hole in the wall automatic teller machine debit card cheque	salary pay slip	rent purchase fees fines debit card credit card cheque

Exercise 2b

The underlined words in the table have the same meaning.

Exercise 2c

1 cash point (or ATM, …)
2 fine
3 fees
4 overdraft
5 mortgage

Exercise 3

1 a
2 b

Part 2 Skills development

Exercise 1

explanation (x 2)	the companies that are quoted in the leading share price indices small and medium-sized enterprises, with less than 250 employees
reason (x 3)	successive governments have sought to encourage small business start-ups forcing entrepreneurs to go through planning steps to make sure their business propositions are viable to make sure that planned products and services meet customer needs
example	new and developing small businesses
comparison	this is up from the previous year and represents the best figures ever recorded
condition	if new entrepreneurs are to succeed, if new businesses are to thrive

Exercise 2a and 2b

i **Paragraph A:** c – the paragraph starts talking about large companies, and the attention that the media gives it, but this is just background information which serves as a contrast to the important information about small businesses that follows.
The topic sentence is: *However, most economists agree that smaller businesses, particularly new and developing small businesses, are crucial to the long-term success of any economy.*

ii **Paragraph D:** b – the topic sentence is *The government also encourages small businesses because they are: …* (The whole paragraph is an extended sentence.)

iii **Paragraph E:** b – the topic sentence is *If new entrepreneurs are to succeed, if new businesses are to thrive, then it is important that they appreciate the central role of planning.*

Exercise 3

1 Which <u>paragraph</u> mentions <u>statistics</u>? B
2 In paragraph <u>A</u>, which <u>word</u> indicates that the text will <u>not</u> be about <u>large businesses</u>?
   However
3 In paragraph <u>C</u>, which <u>sentence</u> explains <u>why new and developing small businesses</u> are <u>crucial</u> to the success of the <u>economy</u>?
   Behind the policy is a belief that small businesses contribute to a stronger economic base, and that they have the ability to thrive in a competitive global business environment.
4 Which <u>paragraph</u> builds on the <u>same idea as</u> the one in <u>A and C</u> (mentioned in question 3)? D

Part 3   Exam practice

1 B
2 F
3 I
4 C
5 G
6 E

Unit 8   Young people's rights

Part 1   Vocabulary

Exercise 1a

a group of people	a person	an object	an activity
council committee	representative member chairperson secretary	minutes	election nomination vote

Note: chairperson is often abbreviated to' chair'.

Exercise 1b

Beech Lane School Parent **Committee/ Council**

Minutes of the meeting held on October, 2012.

Apologies were received from Mrs Smart.

There were two points covered:

1 Because of the long-term absence of Mrs Smart, we will have a/an **election** for a new **chairperson** to lead the meetings. We need all the **nominations** two weeks before the next meeting. Any **member/representative** who attends that meeting will be able to take part in the **voting/election**.

2 The school fair was discussed. A list of duties was drawn up and will be sent to everybody by Friday. It's expected that everyone will do their best to help out on the day.

Exercise 1c

1 council
2 committee
3 secretary
4 minutes
5 chairperson

Exercise 2

1 the <u>photographs</u> of the people partying on the beach with my sisters
2 the <u>importance</u> of the education I received in the UK
3 the <u>details</u> of the cases involving the teenagers who travelled without passports
4 the <u>secret</u> of a successful career

Part 2   Skills development

Exercise 1a

Examples of possible answers:

1 The African Charter on the rights and welfare of the ... = adjective or noun (e.g. *African ... / people ...*)
2 It was chosen ... = preposition or verb (e.g. *by ... / to help ...*)

3 This Children's charter ... = verb (e.g. *has* ...)

4 It covers the economic, social, political and cultural ... = noun (e.g. *issues*)

5 Education needs to be ... = verb, adverb, preposition or adjective (e.g. *encouraged* ... / *efficiently* ... / *for* ... / *good* ...)

6 It needs to be delivered ... = preposition or adverb (e.g. *in* ... / *well* ...)

Exercise 1b

1 c	3 f	5 d
2 a	4 e	6 b

Exercise 2

i c – a is wrong because the idea of 'want' is not in the text. b is wrong: people with disabilities are mentioned because their right may need to improve, but that does not mean that the rights apply to them more than other people.

ii c – a is wrong because the sentence is not grammatical. b is wrong because war does not make human rights less important; war means that people often do not receive their human rights.

iii b – a is wrong because the right to be treated equally in all areas of public life does not have the same meaning as 'accepted everywhere in public'. Sentence c is not grammatical.

iv b – a is wrong because it is the other way around: changes in society and technology resulted in the charter. c is wrong because declarations were updated, not replaced.

v c – a is wrong: the convention covers these rights, but 'should' is not correct. b is wrong: the UK has agreed to follow these rules, which means that they are giving rights to this age group

Part 3   Exam practice

1 G (see introductory paragraph)

2 H ('dress code' refers to 'uniform')

3 E (see point 1 under 'Year councils')

4 D (see point 7 under 'Year councils')

5 C (see last paragraph)

Unit 9   Community matters

Part 1   Vocabulary

Exercise 1

1 centre

2 college

3 policing

4 service

5 care

6 spirit

Exercise 2

communal: adjective: belonging or relating to a community as a whole; something that is shared,

a commune: noun: a group of people who live together and share everything

a communist: noun: a supporter of communism (the political belief that all people are equal and that workers should control the means of producing things)

Exercise 3

	adjective	verb	adverb	noun
criminal	✓	criminalize (note: we say 'to commit' a crime)	criminally	✓
volunteer	voluntary	✓	voluntarily	✓
loyalty	loyal	(verb: 'to be loyal')	loyally	✓
residential	✓	to reside		residence, resident
punish	punished punishable punishing	✓		punishment

Exercise 4

1 a – political party

2 f – online community

3 g – voluntary organization

4 b – film cast

5 c – rock band
6 d – friendship group
7 e – sports team

Part 2   Skills development

Exercise 1

Category 1: meaning (groups)	Category 2: pronouns	Category 3: adjectives
organization	he	educational
community	her	communal
team	they	practical
cast	she	loyal
crowd	theirs	academic
band	them	criminal
party	mine	safe

Exercise 2

Suggested answers:
B new trees
C Oral History / History project / training day
D (events') sponsors / sponsoring
E fountain damage / graffiti damage / minimizing damage
F Forest Schools / Schools activities
G Egg Roll / Easter competition / Egg competition

Exercise 3

1 D
2 A, B, D (sponsoring), G
3 E
4 F, G
5 D, F, G
6 A, D
7 B, C

Exercise 4

1 due to popular demand,
2 There was a huge response to the Forest Schools activities …
3 The first past the finishing line will win a massive chocolate egg!

4 The group will be meeting again and will have the opportunity to do some practice interviews …
5 Lots of new trees have gone in recently.
6 All sessions must be booked in advance …

Part 3   Exam practice

1 A – paragraph 6: *whatever forms communities take … sense … of security*
2 A – paragraph 4: *there are many types of communities in between these extremes,* paragraph 6: *whatever forms communities take*
3 A – paragraph 5: *these groups… larger group… we can feel supported*
4 A – paragraph 1: *'Community' is not a concept that is easy to define;* paragraph 6: *the stereotypical views … may not be completely true… whatever forms communities take …*
5 A – paragraphs 4 and 5: *many examples provided,* and *these groups provide something that we cannot achieve on our own … feel supported in whatever we do*
6 A – paragraph 5: *these groups provide something that we cannot achieve on our own*
7 C – paragraph 3: *… members are unlikely to have actually met each other. These are online communities…*
8 C – paragraph 2: *always someone… look after their children… neighbours …happy to help out… everyone takes responsibility for the welfare of the others*
9 D – paragraph 4: *In reality, of course, this is not true, as the connections are real*

Review 3

Exercise 2

courageous – brave (line 14)
decline – downturn (line 22)
disappearing – drying up (line 12)
encourage – promote (line 17)
first – initial (line 10)
global – multinational/international (line 1 / line 4)
importance – value (line 3)
increasing – growing (line 15)
level – scale (line 3)
vital – important (line 13)

Exercise 3

1 e
2 c
3 a
4 b
5 d

Exercise 4

Check the text on page 66 for the original sentences. The sentences are likely to be followed by:
1 a noun phrase = (article) (adjective) noun)
2 a verb
3 a complete sentence
4 *to* and verb
5 a noun phrase
6 *-ing* form
7 *in* and noun
8 comparative adjective (e.g. *better, higher, more important* …)

Exercise 5

1 In my community, there are **a few** problems with graffiti, but not very many.
2 If one of my students has disorganized notes, I know they will have problems revising. (correct – *they* can refer to an individual)
3 I dislike it when I have to use a communal bathroom. (correct)
4 The customer service assistant who wanted to speak to this customer is not here today, so I have asked the customer to speak to somebody else. (correct – the customer service assistant is not here, so the customer, who is here, will need to speak to somebody else)
5 The person who is standing next to my sister is taller than her, but only because they are wearing a hat. (correct – the person is taller than my sister because *they* (*he* or *she*) is wearing a hat)

Exercise 6

1 rock band
2 community policing / community support officer
3 online community
4 sports team

Unit 10 **British culture**

Part 1 **Vocabulary**

Exercise 1a
1 c
2 a
3 d
4 b

Exercise 1b
1 The Gherkin
2 The Palace of Westminster
3 City Hall
4 The Old Bailey

Exercise 2
1 kettle
2 cup
3 tearoom
4 teapot
5 jam
6 traditions
7 butter
8 sandwiches
9 salmon
10 milk

Exercise 3a

food	drink	activity

rarebit
Cornish
pasty
scones
haggis
leek
	scotch
	bitter
	(a kind
	of beer
	that
	is mid
	brown
	in
	colour)
		hopscotch
		(a children's game which
		    involves jumping between
		    squares which are drawn on
		    the ground)
		duck-duck-goose
		(a circle game based on
		    chasing each other)
		British bulldog
		(a chase game often played in
		    school playgrounds)

Exercise 3b
English: Cornish pasty, from the county of
Cornwall: a small pie which consists of pastry
folded around meat and vegetables; scones
(small bread-like cakes made from flour and
fat, usually eaten with butter).
Welsh: Welsh rarebit: a variation of cheese
on toast; leek: a vegetable which traditionally
symbolizes Wales
Scottish: scotch (whisky), haggis (cooked
sheep's heart, liver and lungs)

Exercise 4

'Great Britain' refers to the countries of
England, Wales and Scotland together.

'The United Kingdom of Great Britain and
Northern Ireland), is usually referred to as 'the
UK', and sometimes as 'Britain'. It consists
of four countries: England, Scotland, Wales
and Northern Ireland. The adjective to refer to
'United Kingdom' is 'British', so we talk about
'British citizens'.

Ireland is an island that consists of Northern
Ireland and the Republic of Ireland.

The British Isles consist of Great Britain,
Ireland and other (smaller) islands, including
the Channel Islands and the Isle of Man.

Part 2 Skills development

Exercise 1a

A

It is <u>not easy to compare the artistic styles and periods of different countries</u>, especially as they may use different words to refer to the same features, and perhaps occasionally also use the same words with a slightly different meaning. Moreover, particular styles and periods overlap.

Exercise 1b

Suggested answers:

B

An example of this is the '<u>Victorian</u>' period in Britain, which has a style that is often described as romantic. First of all, the name of this period links it immediately with British royal history, which potentially creates <u>confusion</u> to <u>non-British people</u> who <u>may not be aware</u> that the reign of Queen Victoria relates to approximately the <u>second half of the 19th century</u>. Secondly, <u>despite</u> the fact that <u>Queen Victoria died in 1901 the style itself continued into the 20th century</u>. And last but not least, it can be argued that there are <u>distinctly different styles which can all be referred to as Victorian</u>, e.g. the use of flower motifs and pastel colours.

C

<u>Despite</u> Victorian times being characterized by <u>romanticism</u>, the famous British <u>romantic poets belong to the period before Queen Victoria</u>. These are poets such as Robert Burns, William Wordsworth, Samuel Taylor Coleridge and John Keats. From the same era date famous writers such as Jane Austen and Mary Shelley (who wrote Frankenstein), and great architects such as James Wyatt and John Nash. The great painters Gainsborough, Reynolds, Turner and

Constable can also be categorized in this period. But who outside of Britain could label this era? And, even if we know they can all be described as <u>Georgian</u> artists, <u>which King George</u> does this refer to? Actually, it refers to <u>four of them</u> (George I, George II, George III and George IV), and thus <u>spans a long period</u> incorporating most of the 18th century and some of the 19th. But <u>then again</u>, there was a <u>Georgian revival</u> in the 20th century, which means the label can also relate to that. Moreover, the style itself <u>incorporates previous styles</u>, including gothic, and has its <u>own subdivision</u>, Regency style, which describes the period of George IV.

D

The period after the Victorian era is referred to as <u>Edwardian</u>, after Edward VII who reigned from 1901 to 1910, when he died. <u>Nobody is sure whether 1910 is the correct end point</u> for the period, with some people suggesting it should be 1912, when the Titanic sank, the start of World War I (1914), its end (1918), or the signing of the post-war peace treaty of Versailles (1919). Elsewhere in Europe, the <u>Art Nouveau era ended around the same time</u>, and unsurprisingly, <u>Art Nouveau</u> is also used to describe the style which was <u>common in Britain</u> at that time. Floral motifs were very common… now where have I heard about that before?

Exercise 1c

first of all (B): introduces the first reason why it is difficult to describe 'Victorian' (you need to be aware of the dates of when British royalty ruled)

secondly (B): gives another reason for the difficulty (the style continued after the end of her reign)

last but not least (B): the last, but also important reason is introduced (different styles could all be referred to as 'Victorian')

despite (C): introduces a contrast (romanticism can refer to Victorian times or the time before)

then again (C): introduces a contrast (Georgian clearly related to the 18th and 19th centuries... but can also refer to the 20th)

moreover (C): another reason for the difficulty in describing what Georgian refers to (it includes previous styles/ and has a subdivision)

unsurprisingly (D): this word indicates that by now the reader will not be surprised to hear that another style (Art Nouveau) is around at the same time as other styles and has elements in common with different styles (e.g. floral motifs, which were also around in Victorian times)

Exercise 1d
B: Victorian, C: Georgian (also mentioned: Georgian revival, gothic, Regency), D: Edwardian (and Art Nouveau)

Exercise 1e
Point d is unsuitable: conclusions should not include new information. The other ideas are very relevant in the conclusion. Point a is essential: the conclusion should pick up the main point. Point b is important as referring back to the main ideas brings the text together. Points c and e emphasize the relevance of the text as they link the issue that is explained in the text to real-life consequences.

Exercise 2
Beaumaris:
a **Beaumaris: a castle of contrasts** (beautiful, but actually military, built fast but not finished). b is incorrect: we know it is medieval, but we do not know if it is typical of the style. c is incorrect: we know that it is old and Welsh, but we do not know if it is the oldest one

Edinburgh:
c **Edinburgh Castle and its many roles** – a is incorrect: this question is not really asked or answered, although clearly there is a suggestion that it is a very old castle (*all the way back to* ...). b is incorrect: the fact that Scotland is proud is mentioned, but the paragraph does not develop this point.

Part 3   Exam practice
Section A: ii
Section B: x
Section C: iii
Section D: v
Section E: i
Section F: vii

Unit 11   Crime detection

Part 1   Vocabulary
Exercise 1
1 candlestick
2 rope
3 lead pipe
4 spanner

Exercise 2a

| 1 d | 3 g | 5 b | 7 c |
| 2 h | 4 f | 6 e | 8 a |

Exercise 2b

| i a | iii c | v c | vii b |
| ii a | iv b | vi a | |

Exercise 2c
Suggested answers:
1 keep your nose clean
2 daylight robbery
3 got away with murder
4 face the music
5 a slap on the wrist
6 above board
7 did a runner
8 a steal

Exercise 3

closing time: this normally refers to the time pubs close

Part 2 Skills development

Exercise 1

1 NOT GIVEN – you may know that this is true, or be able to guess it, but the sentence does not mention that computers were used to date the fingerprints.
2 ✓ – *date back thousands of years to the time of the ancient Egyptians*
3 NOT GIVEN – he probably is, as he seems to have a French name, and he set up a laboratory in France, but this is not actually stated
4 ✓ – *Lyons in France*
5 ✓ – we know that it is technically possible in 1990 as the sentence says that it was already possible in the 1980s – we do not need to use our own knowledge or guess
6 ✓ – somebody who is convicted for murder has been found guilty of murder

Exercise 2

1 TRUE – the abbreviation is given in brackets after the phrase that has the same meaning
2 NOT GIVEN – it may seem obvious to most people that recording and collecting evidence is important police work, but the statement does not mention that it is important
3 NOT GIVEN – the text only says that they record and collect evidence
4 NOT GIVEN – you may feel that being available day and night and remaining at work for weeks is difficult, but this is not in the text
5 FALSE
6 NOT GIVEN – this is unlikely, but all we know is that they stay until all the evidence is collected
7 TRUE
8 NOT GIVEN – reconstructions are mentioned, but we do not know if these involve actors
9 TRUE

Exercise 3

Part 1

Paragraph 1: False – only 1 in 14
Paragraph 2: True – it is 'helpful' in solving small (shoplifting and car crime) and larger crimes (terrorism and murder are both mentioned)
Paragraph 3: True – a *decade* is a period of ten years

Part 2

Paragraph 1: True – *false sense of security, careless*
Paragraph 2: True – *CCTV alone makes no positive impact ... unless you have lots of other things in place ... should ... be focusing on how to alter the environment*
Paragraph 3: True – *have recently begun experimenting with cameras in their helmets*

Part 3 Exam practice

1 FALSE – they are kept apart, not together
2 TRUE – a police officer will arrive first
3 NOT GIVEN – we know that they try to avoid this from happening but we don't know if it sometimes does
4 FALSE – it is photographed four times
5 TRUE
6 NOT GIVEN – there is a suggestion that special procedures may be able to save some burnt evidence but we cannot be sure that this is what 'special procedures' refers to
7 TRUE – *SOCOs ...standard methods ... provide valid information that can be used, or be admissible, in court... The way in which the SOCO team searches for, collects, packages and stores such evidence is important in preserving it...*
8 NOT GIVEN

Unit 12 Travel

Part 1 Vocabulary

Exercise 1
1 country lane
2 motorway
3 path
4 dual carriageway

Exercise 2
Correct words:
1 motorway
2 path
3 dual carriageway
4 country lane

Exercise 3a

commuter101 Is anybody else fed up with road works? Is it just <u>here in London</u> where they are appearing all at once, or is it the same <u>everywhere</u>? It's added an hour to my journey. EACH WAY.

Heather98 Pretty much the same here, commuter 101. I have to do a round trip of 20 miles between <u>Cheltenham</u> and <u>Birmingham</u> every day and pass (very slowly!) 3 areas with road works, on different parts of the M5. It's doubling the time it takes me to get to and from my <u>place of work</u>.

Musicfan2 Take a train, guys. Last time I checked trains were going regularly between <u>Cheltenham</u> and <u>Birmingham</u>. And in <u>London</u> you've got the tube.

CharlotteL. It's driving me crazy too. There are road works near the service station by Junction 9 on the M6. It's like the traffic is at a standstill there. I try to avoid it but it's not always possible.

Heather98 @ Musicfan2: not an option, I'm afraid. I am a sales rep and need my car for other journeys during the day.

chico I agree with Musicfan. Instead of complaining about road works, the cost of petrol, the price of cars etc. we need to think about other options. And I don't mean car sharing or building more motorways. I say we try to save our environment by campaigning for better bus and train networks and for different types of public transport such as trams. Use your time and anger to try and make a difference!

commuter101 What time? I'm stuck in a traffic jam!! (☺)

Exercise 3b
1 fed up	6 a junction
2 pretty much	7 a standstill
3 a round trip	8 rep
4 M5, M6	9 campaigning
5 service station	

Exercise 4

Formal or neutral	Informal
to commute	to be fed up
almost	pretty much
a campaign	a rep
options	guys
anger	
a junction	

Exercise 5
1 c	3 d
2 b	4 a

Part 2 Skills development

Exercise 1
1 fact	4 opinion	7 opinion
2 fact	5 fact	
3 fact	6 fact	

Exercises 2a and 2b

Paragraph 1

1 NO – *people feel reassured…? Possibly. But most of them, especially visitors to the UK, may feel that there is something to worry about…*

2 YES – *the police, armed or not, cannot protect us from bombers*

3 YES – *… police … sometimes … make mistakes … worse when there are firearms involved*

4 YES – *arming police may do more harm than good*

Paragraph 2

5 NO – *instead of complaining …*

6 NO – *try to save our environment*

7 YES – *try… campaigning for better bus and train networks and … trams*

Paragraph 3

8 YES – *the rise in fuel prices is a very worrying trend*

9 YES – *Here are just some examples of the consequences*

10 YES – *The prices of food … also increase as a direct result of the cost of oil, e.g. … beef*

11 NO – it is true that the environment may benefit: *there is one possible advantage …* but *… surely, this is not enough*

12 YES – *What we need is … to reduce fuel prices and/or financially support those who are being affected*

Exercise 3

1 NOT GIVEN

2 ✓ – people lose their jobs because they can no longer afford to commute to work

3 ✓ – *… rely on their own transport for work,* e.g. delivery people

4 NOT GIVEN – only the prices of *some* foods are related to the price of oil, we know about cotton but not about corn

5 ✓ – according to the text, they do not exist yet: *employing more people to design fuel-efficient cars, which will benefit …*

6 NOT GIVEN – saying that *we need … political goodwill … to reduce fuel prices* is not the same as saying that *politicians are not working hard enough*

Part 3   Exam practice

1 YES – *popularly known as the silk road*

2 NOT GIVEN – this is likely, but not stated in the text

3 YES – *Zhang Qian, the Chinese ambassador-adventurer*

4 NOT GIVEN – this is likely, but we do not know that the person who used the name first also used the road

5 NOT GIVEN – this is likely because of its name, but the text does not say it is the main material

6 YES – examples are given of natural materials, e.g. *gems*; man-made materials, e.g. *glass*, and animals: *livestock* is mentioned

7 NO – the text says that he was the first Chinese person to do so, but that it is not certain that others did not go hundreds of years earlier, e.g. the Romans

8 YES – *may well* expresses a probability, but not absolute certainty

9 NO – the writer suggests that this is not evidence as *its exact location remains uncertain* and that the truth about the tower is unknown: *Whatever the truth about the Stone Tower may be …*

10 NOT GIVEN – The city would have been a welcome sight for travellers, and they would probably have been welcome because they were doing trade, but none of this is said in the text

11 NOT GIVEN – this is what the name suggests, but this is just a name, and not necessarily a fact

12 YES – *It is unlikely that in these earlier times traders or travellers would have continued further eastwards from Kashgar, … there still would have remained eight hundred miles of a dangerous journey before they would have found the first true signs of Chinese civilization.*

Review 4

Exercise 2
1 administrative
2 daily
3 traditional
4 Cornish
5 British
6 geographical
7 Victorian
8 Edwardian
9 Georgian

Exercise 3
1 to keep your nose clean
2 to get a slap on the wrist
3 to face the music
4 to be above board
5 to get away with murder
6 it's daylight robbery

Exercise 4
Beaumaris castle is an impressive medieval castle. It was built by King Edward I and is considered one of the most beautiful Edwardian castles in Wales, probably because of its symmetrical shapes, but its purpose was military. Work started in 1295, but although it was done at a fast speed, it was never completed because of lack of money.

Scotland is right to be proud of Edinburgh castle. It dominates the city of Edinburgh from high up on its rock. The history of Castle Rock goes back all the way to the late Bronze Age (900 BC), when there were already people living there. It is now mainly known as a visitor attraction. Although it is more expensive than other tourist attractions, people visit it because it offers excellent value.

Exercise 5
A iv: Crime fighting with technology
B vi: The use of CCTV cameras
C ii: Is CCTV really effective?
D i: Making CCTV effective

Note:
iii: How CCTV works: this heading is incorrect as this topic is not mentioned
v: The fight against terrorism: *terrorism* is mentioned in B but is not central to the paragraph
vii: The police and their opinion: a police report is mentioned in C, but this is only one element in the paragraph. The last sentence in C demonstrates that it is about conflicting evidence with regard to effectiveness.

Exercise 6
1 YES – they are not Victorian, they belong to the period before Victoria's rule
2 NOT GIVEN – they may have known each other because they lived in the same period, but there is no evidence provided for this
3 YES – it can, but it can also refer to the three other kings named George
4 NO – gothic is referred to as a 'previous' style to Georgian, which is incorporated into Georgian
5 NOT GIVEN – there is a style that refers to the period when he rules, but we do not know if he himself had style

Practice test

1 YES – *both in number and size*

2 NOT GIVEN – the connection between finance and confidence is made, but the fact that online shopping is cheaper is not mentioned

3 YES – *shopping is becoming a leisure activity as much as a necessity*

4 YES – *This can result in young people feeling that they are being victimized and forced out of city centres*

5 NO – *many High streets have few individual characteristics*

6 YES – *Services are perhaps more resilient ... growth of coffee shops and nail bars ... going against the general trend*

7 a – *'To Let', decline in smaller stores, empty shops in most town centres*

8 a – *The High Street faces real competition*

9 b – *steady growth of supermarkets, the supermarkets continue to grow, large number of planning applications*

10 b – *out on the edges of our towns ... supermarkets ... they've got the town centre surrounded*

11 b – *High Street faces ... also the growing trend for people to shop online*

12 a – *are one part of the issue* [that independent retailers struggle more than the chain stores]

13 d – *very important to secure ... the big names that can guarantee customers*

14 b – *growth of ... nail bars*

15 vii – *has already been forced ... to reduce traffic congestion*

16 vi – *a very low average speed for traffic on London's roads*

17 iii – *joined a growing list of cities ... Copenhagen, Barcelona, Paris ...*

18 i – *Tube map ... has been much copied and adapted elsewhere*

19 v – not iv: 'the best' suggests in all areas, not just *most satisfying 'cultural experience'*

20 iii – not ii: congestion is mentioned, but pollution is not in the text at all, the only traffic mentioned in this paragraph is road traffic

21 i – 'actions' refers to *measures to reduce traffic congestion*

22 viii – 'initiative' relates to *latest solution* – this is not an original idea but it is a new initiative for London

23 vi – benefits include seeing the streets and finding their way around, exercise and possible weight loss

24 solution

25 advertising

26 extensions

27 chip

28 at the weekend

29 parking further/ parking further away

30 life not regular/ not as regular

31 do some skipping/ do skipping

32 outdoors

33 run/ a run

34 F – the paragraph does suggest having a cup of tea and reading the article again, but these are not long activities and the main message of the paragraph is *get up, get going, and don't stop*

35 B – if you do something for six weeks it becomes a habit, so it becomes 'long term', the paragraph also talks about the *right type*, or 'suitable', exercise

36 D – this paragraph is about fitness, and it suggests this can be worked out outdoors and at home

37 a calmer style

38 (your) local council

39 TRUE – see paragraph B

40 NOT GIVEN – in paragraph F, a cup of tea is suggested, but it is not stated why

Glossary

Key

abbr. = abbreviation
adj. = adjective
adv. = adverb
n. = noun
phrasal v. = phrasal verb
phr. = phrase
v. = verb

Unit 1

adult **n.** – a person who is no longer a child

advice **n.** – If you give someone advice, you tell them what you think they should do.

barbecue **n.** – an outdoor party where people cook and eat food

board game **n.** – an indoor game played on a board, usually with pieces that are moved around it, for example chess

camp site **n.** – a place where you can stay on holiday in a caravan or a tent

cards **n.** – a game played with cards that have pictures and numbers on them

chat **n.** – an informal, friendly conversation

close **adj.** – A close relationship or friendship is one in which you know each other well and like each other a lot.

deep **adj.** – A deep relationship is one in which you have strong feelings for each other.

dissatisfaction **n.** – unhappiness

fight **n.** – a quarrel, dispute or contest

gadget **n.** – a small machine that does something useful

guidelines **n.** – rules or advice about how to do something

hang out **v.** – to spend time in a particular place or with particular people, usually friends

have something in common – to have the same interests or opinions as another person or people

hiking **n.** – the activity of going on long walks in the country, especially for pleasure

keep in touch – to continue to write, phone or visit someone although you do not see them often

kick boxing **n.** – a type of boxing in which the opponents are allowed to kick as well as punch each other

leisure **n.** – time when you are not working and you can relax and do things you enjoy

picnic **n.** – a meal you eat outside, usually in a field or forest, or at the beach

poker **n.** – a card game that people play, usually in order to win money

possession **n.** – something that you own

puzzle **n.** – a picture on cardboard or wood that has been cut up into odd shapes that have to be put back together again

quiz **n.** – a game in which you have to answer questions

recent **adj.** – having appeared, happened or been made not long ago

research **n.** – work to collect information on a subject

rules **n.** – instructions, often in writing, telling you what you can and cannot do

share **v.** – to give each person in a group a fair or equal part of something

shopping centre **n.** – a large building that contains a lot of shops

social networking site **n.** – a website that allows people to communicate with their friends or with people who have similar interests

socialize (with) **v.** – If you socialize with people, you meet them socially, for example at parties.

spend time **v.** – to pass time in a specific way, activity, place, etc.

stranger **n.** – any person you do not know

temporary **adj.** – for a limited time, not forever

value **v.** – If you value someone or something, you think that they are important and you appreciate them.

weightlifting **n.** – a sport in which people lift heavy weights

woods **n.** – a large area of trees that are growing closely together

Unit 2

carry out **v.** – If you carry out a task, you do it.

concept **n.** – an idea

cope **v.** – If you cope with a situation or problem, you deal with it successfully.

disability **n.** – the condition of being unable to use a part of the body or brain because of a physical or mental injury

find **v.** – used to express your reaction to something you have experienced

genetic **adv.** – biologically given from parents to children

height **n.** – the vertical distance from the bottom of something to the top

huge **adj.** – extremely large

illness **n.** – a disease or sickness

impact upon **v.** – to affect a situation, process or person

implication **n.** – something that is likely to happen as a result of something, a consequence

in terms of – If you talk about something **in terms of** something, you are specifying from what point of view you are considering it.

income **n.** – money you receive, usually from working or from investments

issue **n.** – a situation or subject that people are talking about

lead to **v.** – If something leads to a situation or event, it causes it to happen.

likely **adj.** – used to say that something will probably happen

limitation **n.** – If someone has limitations, they can only do some things and not others, or they cannot do something very well.

link (to) **v.** – If one thing is linked to another thing, there is a relationship or connection between them.

lose weight **v.** – to become thinner or less heavy

moreover **conj.** – in addition to what has already been said

neighbourhood **n.** – one of the parts of a town where people live

nevertheless **conj.** – in spite of something you have just said; however

noticeable **adj.** – Something that is noticeable is easy to see, hear or recognize.

obese **adj.** – extremely fat

poverty **n.** – the condition of being poor and without adequate food, etc.

processed **adj.** – prepared in factories

promote **v.** – to encourage something

range (of) **n.** – a series or number of different items

risk **n.** – the possibility of something bad happening

shuttlecock **n.** – the object that you hit over the net in a game of badminton

success **n.** – the achievement of something you have been trying to do (*successful* **adj.**)

survey **n.** – a set of questions that you ask a large number of people or organizations

symptom **n.** – something wrong with your body or mind that is a sign of an illness

tend (to) **v.** – to usually do something

valuation **n.** – an opinion that someone has about how much the value of something is, what it is worth

vary **v.** – to be different for different people or situations

wellbeing **n.** – the condition of being contented, healthy or successful

Unit 3

6th form college – an educational institution where students aged 16 to 19 typically study for advanced school-level qualifications

ambitious **adj.** – having a strong desire for success or achievement; wanting power, money, etc.

bachelor's degree **n.** – a university degree awarded for an undergraduate course

benefit from **v.** – to get an advantage from something

broaden **v.** – to make or become broader or wider

elaborate on **v.** – to add information or detail to something that has been said

engineering **n.** – the profession of designing and constructing engines and machinery or structures such as roads or bridges

enhance **v.** – to improve the quality or value of something

equivalent **adj.** – equal in value, quantity, significance, etc.

fluent **adj.** – able to speak or write a foreign language very well

foreign **adj.** – coming from another country

have (things) in common – to resemble one another in specific ways

infant school **n.** – a school for children aged between 5 and 7

lasting **adj.** – permanent or enduring

law **n.** – a rule or set of rules, enforceable by the courts

like-minded **adj.** – Like-minded people have similar opinions, attitudes, interests, etc.

master's degree **n.** – a university degree for further studies after the first/bachelor's degree

nursery school **n.** – a school for young children, usually from three to five years old

on site **adj.** – done or located at the site of a particular activity, etc.

ongoing **adj.** – happening now and likely to continue

overseas **adv.** – in or to foreign countries

PhD **abbr.** – Doctor of Philosophy, the highest university degree

primary school **n.** – a school for children below the age of 11. It is usually divided into an infant and a junior section

procedure **n.** – a way of doing something, especially an established method

proof **n.** – any evidence that shows that something is true

rank **v.** – to put things in position according to importance, size, etc.

recall **v.** – to remember something

research **n.** – work done to discover facts about something

secondary school **n.** – a school for young people, usually between the ages of 11 and 18

submit **v.** – to refer something to someone who will make a decision about it

support **n.** – help and kindness given to someone who is in a difficult situation

translation **n.** – something that is or has been changed into a different language

welcoming **adj.** – friendly, especially with visitors, guests, etc.

Unit 4

add **v.** – to put something with something else

appliance **n.** – a machine or device, especially an electrical one used in the home

atmosphere **n.** – the air surrounding the earth or any other planet

button **n.** – a small object you press to make a machine or device work

circuit board **n.** – a board with electronic connections inside a computer, mobile phone, etc.

coat **v.** – to cover something with a layer of something

connotations **n.** – The connotations of a word or phrase are the ideas or qualities that it makes you think of.

conservation **n.** – the protection or careful use of something so that it lasts for a long time

corrode **v.** – If something corrodes, it is gradually destroyed by a chemical action.

distillation **n.** – the process of evaporating or boiling a liquid and condensing its vapour

fall **v.** – to move downwards

fermentation **n.** – a chemical change in which food or a natural substance produces alcohol

fold **v.** – to bend or be bent double so that one part covers another

guess **v.** – to give an answer or opinion that may not be correct because you do not know enough information

harmful **adj.** – causing or likely to cause damage

icing **n.** – a sweet substance made from powdered sugar, used for decorating cakes, biscuits, etc.

keyboard **n.** – the set of keys that you press to make a computer, mobile phone, etc. work

liquid crystal display **n.** – a flat-screen display used, for example, in portable computers, mobile phones, etc.

mixture **n.** – a combination of different things

operating system **n.** – the set of software that controls the way a computer system works

refuse (to do something) **v.** – to say you will not do something

replacement **n.** – something that you use instead of something else

rise **v.** – to move upwards

sailor **n.** – a member of a ship's crew

source **n.** – the place or thing that you get something from

surface **n.** – the top or outside part of something

surround **v.** – to be all around something

waste **n.** – the use of something in a way that is not necessary

whatsoever **adv.** – used to emphasize a negative statement

Unit 5

bark **n.** – the hard substance on the trunk of a tree

beneficial **adj.** – Something that is beneficial helps people or improves their lives.

breastfeed **v.** – to feed a baby with milk from the breast

coastal **adj.** – on the land that is next to the sea

crab **n.** – a type of shellfish with ten legs that walks sideways

crystallize **v.** – to become a crystal (= a substance that forms naturally into a regular symmetrical shape)

current **n.** – a strong movement of water in a particular direction

deserve **v.** – If you deserve something, you should have it because of your actions or qualities.

deter **v.** – to discourage or prevent something from happening

forehead **n.** – the part of the face above the eyes and below the hairline

frost **n.** – a thin layer of ice particles that form at night on things outside when it is very cold

garnish **n.** – something that is used to decorate food, e.g. a herb

gelatinous **adj.** – wet and sticky

ground **adj.** – broken up into very small pieces of powder

gum **n.** – a sticky substance that comes out of some plants

jellyfish **n.** – a soft, translucent sea animal with an umbrella-shaped body with trailing tentacles that sting

layer **n.** – a thickness of a substance that covers a surface

livestock **n.** – animals such as cattle, sheep and hens that are kept on a farm

marine **adj.** – related to the sea, e.g. the animals and plants that live there

outdoor pursuits **n.** – activities that you do outside in countryside, such as hill walking, trekking, canoeing, kayaking, rafting, climbing, caving

pickled **adj.** – Pickled food is kept in vinegar or sea water to preserve it.

properties **n.** – the qualities or features that something has

publish **v.** – to produce copies of a book or magazine etc. for distribution and sale

relieve **v.** – to reduce pain, distress, etc.

rot **v.** – to decay gradually

shallow **adj.** – measuring only a small distance from the top to the bottom of a liquid, not deep

sink **v.** – to move down under the surface of a liquid or soft substance

skeleton **n.** – the set of bones that forms a human or animal body

sting **v.** – If an insect, animal or plant stings you, it makes your skin hurt because a sharp part of it, often covered in poison, is pushed into your skin.

stir-fry **n.** – a Chinese dish made by cooking small pieces of meat and vegetables in very hot oil

stomach complaint **n.** – a pain or medical problem of the stomach

surrounding **adj.** – near or all around a place

swollen **adj.** – If part of your body is swollen, it is larger than normal, usually because of an illness or injury.

thrive **v.** – If a plant thrives, it grows very well.

tide **n.** – the cyclic rise and fall of sea level caused by the gravitational pull of the sun and moon. There are usually two high tides and two low tides in each lunar day

treasure trove **n.** – a collection or source of valuable objects

wash up **v.** – If the sea washes something up, it carries an object onto a beach and leaves it there.

Welsh **adj.** – relating to Wales

Unit 6

achieve **v.** – If you achieve a particular aim or effect, you succeed in making it happen.

agenda **n.** – a list of subjects that will be discussed at a meeting

argue **v.** – to give the reasons for your opinion, idea, etc.

clue **n.** – something that helps to solve a problem or unravel a mystery

coach **v.** – to teach people a special skill

cogently **adv.** – If you argue something cogently, you give good and convincing reasons.

conflict **n.** – disagreement and argument

convey **v.** – to communicate a message or information

decode **v.** – to convert a message, text, etc. from code into ordinary language

dispute **n.** – an argument or disagreement

drag on **v.** – You say that an event or process drags on when you disapprove of the fact that it lasts for longer than necessary.

draw out **v.** – to pull out or extract

encourage **v.** – to give someone confidence and make them want to do something

engage in **v.** – to take part in a particular activity, especially one that involves competing or talking to other people

facial **adj.** – of or relating to the face

formal **adj.** –following correct or established official methods or style

forum **n.** – a situation or place in which people exchange ideas and discuss issues

gesture **n.** – a movement that you make with a part of your body to express information

greet **v.** – If something greets you, it is the first thing you notice.

handy **adj.** – conveniently or easily within reach

interpersonal **adj.** – involving personal relationships between people

intonation **n.** – the sound pattern of your voice as you speak

layout **n.** – the way in which something appears or is arranged

podcast **n.** – an audio file similar to a radio broadcast, which can be downloaded and listened to on a computer, mp3 player, mobile phone, etc.

role **n.** – the part played by a person in a particular situation

season **n.** – a period of time when something takes place or happens

small talk **n.** – light conversation for social occasions

sneak **v.** – to move quietly and secretly

solve **v.** – to find the explanation for or solution to a mystery, problem, etc.

summarize **v.** – to give the most important points from a speech, report, etc. in a short and clear way

supplier **n.** – an organization or person that provides goods or a service to others

surf the Web – to look at several websites on the Internet

take for granted **v.** – If you say that someone takes you for granted, you are complaining that they benefit from your help, efforts or presence without showing that they are grateful.

title **n.** – a word (usually abbreviated) used before someone's name, e.g. Mr, Ms, Mrs, Miss

to the point – If something you say or write is to the point, it is relevant and does not include unnecessary details.

trade union official **n.** – a person who works for an organization that represents workers and helps to improve working conditions and wages

trade **v.** – to buy and sell things

turn into **v.** – to change into something different

volume **n.** – the intensity of sound; loudness

anxious **adj.** – slightly worried

argue **v.** – to try to prove something by giving reasons

carry out **v.** – If you carry out a task, you do it.

commitment **n.** – determination or enthusiasm to do something

current legislation **n.** – the most recent laws

delegate **v.** – to give duties, powers, etc. to another person

determine **v.** – to settle or decide an argument, question, etc. conclusively

draw on **v.** – to use something such as skills or knowledge

encourage **v.** – to give someone confidence and make them want to do something

ensure **v.** – to make certain or sure; guarantee

entrepreneur **n.** – a person who sets up businesses and business deals

enterprise **n.** – a company or business, often a small one

failure **n.** – the lack of success

flexible **adj.** – able to change easily and adapt to different situations

foster **v.** – to promote the growth or development of something

gap (in market) **n.** – a situation in which there is something missing from a market, and a new product or service could be sold

high-profile **adj.** – attracting a lot of attention or publicity

innovative **adj.** – using or showing new methods, ideas, etc.

lack **v.** – to not have any or not have enough of something

let go of **v.** – to stop holding something

long-term **adj.** – lasting, staying or extending over a long time

meet someone's needs **v.** – to provide what someone needs

mentor **n.** – an experienced person who gives help and advice to someone else over a period of time

mutually **adv.** – in a way that is experienced or felt by both people or groups involved

originate **v.** – to start to exist

paperwork **n.** – work that involves writing reports, dealing with letters, filling in forms, etc.

run (a business) **v.** – to be in charge of; manage

sales leads **n.** – the identity of people interested in buying a product or service, the first stage of a sales process

set up **v.** – to start a new business

step back **v.** – to stop for a moment in order to consider something or look at something in a different way

success **n.** – the achievement of something you have been trying to do

successive **adj.** – happening or existing one after another without a break

think ahead **v.** – to make plans about the future, so that you will be prepared

thrive **v.** – to do well and be successful

time frame **n.** – the period of time in which something is planned to happen

trading hours **n.** – the hours during which business is open

trust **v.** – to believe that someone will do something well and in the way you want

undermine **v.** – to make something less strong or successful

undertake **v.** – to do something

viable **adj.** – If a plan, suggestion, etc. is viable, it is practical and could be successful.

Unit 8

absence **n.** – the fact that someone is away or not present

agenda **n.** – a list of subjects to be discussed at a meeting

aim **n.** – something you want to achieve

ban **n.** – an official statement saying that something is not allowed

bullying **n.** – hurting people (usually weaker or smaller), especially to make them do something

career **n.** – a profession or series of jobs that someone does for a long time

charity fundraising **n.** – the work of asking people to give money to an organization that helps people

cloning **n.** – the process of creating an exact genetic copy of an animal or plant

deal with **v.** – to take action on

do your best – to try as hard as you can

draw up a list – to prepare and write a list

fair trial **n.** – a fair and public meeting in a law court, in which a judge and jury decide whether someone is guilty of a crime

forum **n.** – a place for discussion

get involved in – to take part in an activity

hunger **n.** – the situation when people do not have enough food to eat

i.e. **abbr.** – that is to say, in other words

improve **v.** – to make something better

keep records – to keep a written account of events or facts

legal framework **n.** – a system of rules, laws, agreements, etc. that establish the way that something operates

let someone know **v.** – to tell someone something

mentor **v.** – to give help and advice over a period of time to someone who has less experience than you

obey rules **n.** – to do what rules say you must do

peer **n.** – a person who is the same age or has the same social or professional position

raise an issue – to mention something that you want people to discuss

resolve conflicts **v.** – to bring disagreements to an end

safeguard **n.** – a rule or law that is intended to protect someone from harm or danger

scheme **n.** – a plan for achieving something

settlement **n.** – the process of reaching an agreement

take account of / take into account – to consider something

take minutes – to write an official record of what is discussed at a meeting

take responsibility for **v.** – to agree that you will do something as part of your job or duty

take up a matter **v.** – to begin to deal with a situation or problem

thorough **adj.** – done completely and carefully

torture **v.** – to cause extreme physical pain to someone, especially in order to get information, etc.

underlying belief **n.** – the belief that something is based on, which may not be obvious

update **v.** – to change something by adding new information or more modern features

welfare **n.** – health, happiness, prosperity, and well-being in general

Unit 9

ably **adv.** – in a competent or skilful way

beech **n.** – a type of tree

campaign **v.** – to try to achieve a social, political or commercial goal by persuading people or a government to do something

cast **n.** – all the actors in a play, film, etc.

come across **v.** – to meet or find someone or something by accident

develop a relationship **v.** – to begin to feel a connection with someone

draw conclusions **v.** – to decide what is true after considering the facts

enrol **v.** – to register your name on an official list to become a member

estate agent **n.** – someone whose job is to value and sell houses for people

finishing line **n.** – the line you have to cross to finish a race

fundraising **n.** – activities to raise money for a good purpose, charity, etc.

give some thought to **v.** – to think about something

hard-boiled egg **n.** – an egg that is cooked in boiling water until the yolk and white are solid

lap **n.** – one circuit of a racecourse or track

like-minded **adj.** – Like-minded people have similar opinions, attitudes, interests, etc.

loyal **adj.** – willing to support someone even in difficult times

meadow **n.** – a field with grass and flowers growing in it

newsletter **n.** – a set of printed sheets of paper containing information about an organization, which is regularly sent to its members

oak **n.** – a type of large tree that can live for a very long time and produces small hard fruits called acorns

political party **n.** – an organization that has or wants to have political power

prison **n.** – a building where criminals are kept as a punishment

punishment **n.** – a penalty or sanction given for any crime or offence

rely on **v.** – to trust someone to do something

sponsor **v.** – to give money for an event, etc., in return for advertising your company

strength in numbers – the fact that a group of people has more power than one person

take place **v.** – to happen

trigger images **v.** – to make you have particular pictures in your mind

unpaid **adj.** – Unpaid work is work that you do not get paid for.

volunteer **n.** – a person who works without receiving any payment

Unit 10

back and forth **adv.** – moving first in one direction and then in the opposite direction many times

ban **v.** – to say officially that someone is not allowed to do something

blame **v.** – to say that you think someone is responsible for something bad that has happened

brew **v.** – If you brew tea or coffee, you make it by pouring hot water over tea leaves or ground coffee.

Bronze Age **n.** – a period of ancient history from around 3500 to 1500 BC

conservatory **n.** – a greenhouse, or room with glass walls, especially one attached to a house

custom **n.** – an activity or way of behaving that is usual or traditional in a particular place or a particular period in history

dungeon **n.** – a closed prison cell, often underground, that was common in old castles

forbid **v.** – to order that something must not be done

gatehouse **n.** – a building above or beside an entrance gate to a city, university, etc.

germ **n.** – a very small organism that can make you sick or ill

go back to **v.** – If something goes back to a particular time in history, it started to exist at that time.

host **v.** – to organize or arrange a special event for guests and be in charge of it

improvement **n.** – work done on something to make it better

injury **n.** – physical damage or hurt

justification **n.** – reason

knot **v.** – to tie a piece of string, rope, etc.

lack of **n.** – a situation in which there is not enough of something

landscape artist **n.** – a painter of areas of natural beauty, especially in the countryside

lawyer **n.** – someone whose job is to advise people about the law and represent them in court

leather **n.** – animal skin that has been made smooth and flexible, often used for making shoes, clothes, furniture, etc.

loose tea **n.** – dried cut leaves of a tea plant that are not in little bags

marbles **n.** – a children's game played with small balls, usually made of coloured glass, in which you roll a ball along the ground and try to hit an opponent's ball

mayor **n.** – an elected civic leader in a town or city

medieval **adj.** – of, relating to, or in the style of the Middle Ages

mound **n.** – a raised mass of earth, etc.

overlap **v.** – If two styles, periods, etc. overlap, they have some of the same features, times, etc. as each other.

peace treaty **n.** – an agreement marking the end of a war

rampart **n.** – the surrounding embankment of a castle or fort, including any walls, etc. that are built to protect it

reign **n.** – the time when a particular king or queen is the ruler of a country

revival **n.** – a time when something becomes popular again

scone **n.** – a light cake made from flour and very little fat, cooked in an oven, usually cut open and buttered

span **v.** – If something spans a long period of time, it relates to that whole period of time.

split your lip **v.** – to injure your mouth and make your lip bleed

string **n.** – a thin length of cord or very thin rope, used for tying or hanging something

sue **v.** – If you sue someone, you start a legal case against them, usually in order to claim money from them because they have harmed you in some way.

swing **v.** – to make something move backwards and forwards

tackle **n.** – an attempt to take the ball away from another player in a game such as rugby, football, hockey, etc.

teapot **n.** – a container with a lid, spout and handle, used for making and serving tea

visitor attraction **n.** – a place that tourists like to visit

wrap **v.** – to fold or wind something around something else

admissible **adj.** – If evidence or information is admissible, it is allowed in a court of law.

alter **v.** – to change something

assess **v.** – to consider and judge or evaluate something

charge with a crime **v.** – to formally accuse someone of committing a crime

assume **v.** – to think, sometimes wrongly, that something is true

cigarette butt **n.** – the part of a cigarette that is left when you have finished smoking

commit murder **v.** – to kill someone deliberately

conflicting **adj.** – Conflicting accounts, stories, etc. are different and cannot both be true.

convict **v.** – to prove that someone is guilty of an offence or crime

crime scene **n.** – the place where a crime happened

date back to **phrasal v.** – to be made or begun at a particular time in the past

debate **n.** – a discussion between people who have different opinions about something

decade **n.** – a period of ten years

decay **v.** – to become gradually destroyed because of a natural process

deteriorate **v.** – to become worse in quality

displace **v.** – to make something move from its usual place to another place

distorted **adj.** – changed, reported or represented in an untrue way

DNA database **n.** – a set of genetic information that can be used to find out if someone has committed a crime, etc.

do the washing **v.** – to wash your clothes

equip to do something **v.** – to provide someone or something with what they need for a particular purpose

evidence **n.** – facts or physical signs on which to base proof or to establish the truth

eyewitness **n.** – a person present at an event who can describe what happened

false sense of security – the mistaken feeling that you are safe

fibre **n.** – a long thin thread from a fabric

fingerprint **n.** – the distinctive mark you leave when you touch something with your finger

footage **n.** – film taken with a camera of a particular event

forensic **adj.** – relating to, used in, or connected with a court of law

fragile **adj.** – able to be broken easily

frozen **adj.** – turned into or covered with ice

have access to **v.** – to have the right to use something or go into a place

helmet **n.** – a protective hat worn by soldiers, policemen, firemen, divers, etc.

in place – working or able to be used

intended **adj.** – planned

label **v.** – to fasten a piece of paper to something, which gives information about the thing

lighting **n.** – lights, street lamps, etc.

naked eye **n.** – If you see something with your naked eye, you do not use a telescope or microscope, etc.

number plate **n.** – the sign on the front and back of all vehicles, that has numbers and letters on it

police force **n.** – the group of police officers in a particular country or area

prevention **n.** – trying to stop something from happening

reveal **v.** – to show something

scale **n.** – a sequence of marks at regular intervals, used as a reference in making measurements

seal **v.** – to close something up so that air cannot get into it

shoplifting **n.** – the act of stealing things from a shop by hiding them in a bag or in clothes

sketch **n.** – a drawing that you do quickly

solve a crime **v.** – to find out who committed a crime and what happened

sophisticated **adj.** – more advanced and using new and clever ideas

suspect **n.** – a person who police think may have committed a crime

systematic **adj.** – done using a fixed plan so that nothing is missed

targeted **adj.** – aimed or directed at a particular person or thing

terrorist **n.** – a person who uses violence, for example bombing a place, for political reasons

thorough **adj.** – done completely and carefully

weight of evidence **n.** – the importance or influence of the facts

Unit 12

ambassador **n.** – an important official who represents a country

at a standstill **n.** – If a place is at a standstill, cars cannot move because there is so much traffic.

award-winning **adj.** – An award-winning product, business or person has won a prize or prizes.

be made redundant **v.** – If you are made redundant, you lose your job because your employer does not need you anymore.

break the speed limit **v.** – to drive faster than the law says you can

exit **v.** – to leave a building or road

firearm **n.** – a gun

fortress **n.** – a strong well-protected building

freeway (Am.) **n.** – a major road that can be used without paying a toll

gem **n.** – a precious or semiprecious stone used in jewellery as a decoration

goodwill **n.** – a feeling of wanting to help someone

literally **adv.** – exactly

livestock **n.** – farm animals

millennia **n.** – plural form of 'millennium': a period of one thousand years

pavement (British – Am. = sidewalk) **n.** – the path for people to walk on next to a road

petrol (Br) **n.** – fuel for a car, etc. *(Am. = gas)*

promenade **n.** - a special place where people can walk, especially at a seaside resort

raw materials **n.** – materials in their natural state, used for a particular manufacturing process

reassured **adj.** – less worried and more confident about something

region **n.** – an area considered as a unit for geographical, functional, social or cultural reasons

rely on **v.** – to depend on something

roadworks **n.** – repairs that are being done to road, especially when this delays traffic

runway **n.** – the long, hard surface at an airport, from which a plane takes off and lands

scholar **n.** – someone who studies an academic subject and knows a lot about it

silk **n.** – a smooth, fine cloth made from fibre produced by a silkworm

slip road **n.** – a short road connecting a motorway, etc. to another road

traffic jam **n.** – a line of vehicles that cannot move because there is so much traffic or because something is blocking the road

tram **n.** – a vehicle that runs on rails on a road, and is powered by electricity from an overhead wire

undertake **v.** – to do something

well worth – If something is well worth doing, there are good reasons to do it.

worrying trend **n.** – a gradual change or development that causes concern or worry

Practice test

blur **v.** – to become less distinct, less clear

brisk **adj.** – lively and quick

clone **v.** – to produce something that is the same or nearly the same as something else

congestion **n.** – the state when there is so much traffic that vehicles cannot move

hub **n.** – the focal point, the centre

iconic **adj.** – well-known and representing a particular belief, nation, etc.

mingle **v.** – to meet and mix with other people

obesity **n.** – the state of being extremely fat

resilient **adj**. – recovering easily and quickly from problems, shock, hardship, etc.

soar **v.** – to increase very quickly

solitary **adj.** – experienced or done alone

supply chain **n.** – a channel of distribution from the maker of materials or components, to the manufacturer, distributor and retailer, and finally to the consumer

tenant **n.** – someone who pays money to the owner of a shop, house, etc. in order to run a business from the shop or live in the house

vacant **adj.** – empty

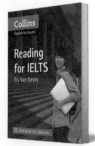 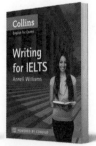 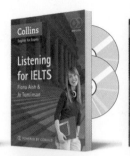

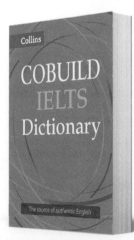